HAUNTED CLARKE COUNTY, VIRGINIA

HAUNTED CLARKE COUNTY, VIRGINIA

MICHAEL D. HESS

Published by Haunted America
A Division of The History Press
Charleston, SC
www.historypress.com

Copyright © 2019 by Michael D. Hess
All rights reserved

Cover images courtesy of the author.

First published 2019

Manufactured in the United States

ISBN 9781467142281

Library of Congress Control Number: 2019943380

Notice: The information in this book is true and complete to the best of our knowledge. It is offered without guarantee on the part of the author or The History Press. The author and The History Press disclaim all liability in connection with the use of this book.

All rights reserved. No part of this book may be reproduced or transmitted in any form whatsoever without prior written permission from the publisher except in the case of brief quotations embodied in critical articles and reviews.

CONTENTS

Acknowledgements   9
Introduction   11

Chapter 1: A Doomed Flight   19
    TWA Flight 514   21
    Paranormal Activity   23
    A Campfire Tale   24
    A Fascinating Ghost Story: Could It Be True?   25

Chapter 2: Haunted Backroads   27
    Wickliffe Road   27
    Stringtown Road   28
    Ebenezer Road   30
    Crums Church Road   33

Chapter 3: Historic Haunts of Berryville   38
    Haunted Historic Homes   40
    The Battletown Inn   43
    Rosemont   46

Chapter 4: The Courthouse Grounds   52

Contents

Chapter 5: Other Berryville Haunts	58
A House on Walnut Street	58
A Hat-Wearing Ghost and a Ghost in a Hoodie	61
Other Haunts	62
Chapter 6: Carter Hall and Long Branch	65
Carter Hall	67
Long Branch	74
Closing Thoughts	77
Chapter 7: Haunts along the River	78
Phantom Soldiers of the Shenandoah River	80
The Chilly Hollow Monster	83
Stubblefield	85
Chapter 8: Slavery and Ghost Lore	88
Runaway Slaves	89
Jerry and Joe	90
Ghost Lore	92
Superstitions	96
Chapter 9: Long Marsh Run to Ephrata: The Story of the Ghostly Beeler Wives	98
Ghostly Manifestations	101
Chapter 10: Other Strange Tales	106
The Smoky Figure	106
The Ghost Likes Your Balloon	108
"He Is Calling Me"	109
A Soldier at the Foot of the Steps	110
An Old-Timey Poltergeist?	111
Afterword	115
Select Bibliography	121
About the Author	125

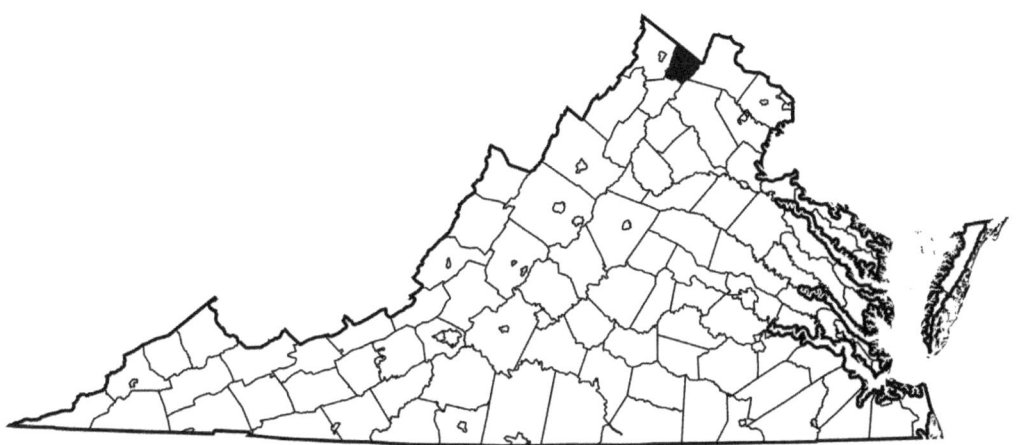

David Benbennick's Virginia map with Clarke County highlighted. *Wikimedia Commons*.

Acknowledgements

First and foremost, I need to thank my wife, Stefanie, a Clarke County girl born and raised, who encouraged me to write this book. Her help in the research was invaluable, and she also took most of the photographs. Her support has been unwavering, and since I started this whole writing thing, she has been my biggest supporter. Stefanie believed in me during those times when I struggled to believe in myself.

I want to thank everyone who shared their stories, passed along tips or helped in any way. There are far too many people to list, but please know that I am grateful, and I thank you all from the bottom of my heart.

Lastly, I have to give a shout out to my editor, Kate Jenkins; copyeditor, Rick Delaney; publicist, Jonny Foster; and all the good folks at The History Press. I cannot thank them enough for taking a chance on me and this book.

INTRODUCTION

Clarke County lies west of the Blue Ridge Mountains in Virginia's magnificent Shenandoah Valley. It is the eighth-smallest county in the commonwealth in terms of land mass, with an area covering only 178 square miles. According to the United States Census, of Virginia's ninety-five counties, Clarke County ranks seventy-third in population, with an estimated 14,508 residents. Being only about 60 miles from Washington, D.C., it is an impressive feat that the county has kept its rural character and small-town feel while other nearby counties have been swallowed up and incorporated into the sprawling, ever-increasing D.C. suburbs. Leaving behind the hustle and bustle of northern Virginia and crossing the mountain into Clarke County, life is much different on the western side. The mountain is a demarcation point between giant tech companies and small family-owned businesses, old Virginia and urban sprawl, congested streets and Main Street.

The Shenandoah River bisects Clarke County; it enters from the southeast at the border with Warren County and flows in a northeasterly direction into Jefferson County, West Virginia, where it dumps into the Potomac River at the Maryland line. Large farms and rolling hills dot the Clarke County landscape, and its mountains are known for their stunning vistas of the Shenandoah Valley.

The first settlement in what would become Clarke County was the estate of Thomas Fairfax, the sixth Lord Fairfax of Cameron. In 1736, he built his home, Greenway Court, at the present-day village of White Post. White

Introduction

"Daughter of the Stars"—the beautiful Shenandoah River bisects Clarke County on its way to the Potomac River. *Courtesy of the author.*

Post takes its name from a white post that directed travelers to Lord Fairfax's estate and land office.

Clarke County was formed in 1836 after the Virginia General Assembly divided Frederick County. It was named in honor of George Rogers Clark, a hero of the American Revolution who helped win the Northwest Territory for Virginia. It is unclear why the name of the county is spelled with an "e" on the end. Interestingly, there are four historical markers in the county that are incorrectly spelled "Clark." Two of the markers are along Route 7, one on U.S. 50 and another on U.S. 522.

The English largely settled the area, and for a time, Clarke County was almost an extension of Tidewater Virginia. The children of the "Tidewater planters" established large, sprawling plantations throughout the county after being issued land grants by Lord Fairfax. The plantation lifestyle flourished here until the War Between the States brought an end to the old way of life. Other Clarke County settlers included Germans and those of Scotch-Irish descent who moved into the area as soaring land prices and overcrowding forced them out of Pennsylvania.

Clarke County lies within the boundary of what came to be known as Mosby's Confederacy during the Civil War. Known today as the Mosby

Introduction

Left: A reproduction of this painting of Lord Fairfax hangs in the lobby of Lord Fairfax Community College in Middletown. *From the Library of Congress Theodor Horydczak Collection.*

Below: Tradition holds that George Washington erected the "White Post" at the intersection of White Post Road and Berrys Ferry Road to direct travelers to the land office and residence of Lord Fairfax. *Courtesy of the author.*

Introduction

A portrait of the "Gray Ghost," Colonel John Singleton Mosby. *From the Library of Congress Civil War Photographs, 1861–1865.*

Heritage Area, this vast stretch of Virginia countryside encompasses 1,800 square miles and includes Loudoun, Fairfax, Fauquier, Clarke, Warren and part of Prince William Counties. The area is named in honor of the "Gray Ghost," Colonel John Singleton Mosby, who commanded the Forty-Third Battalion, Virginia Cavalry, better known as Mosby's Raiders or Mosby's Rangers. The unit was composed of irregular troops recruited under the authority of the Partisan Ranger Act of 1862.

The bulk of Civil War activity in Clarke County took place in 1864, and most engagements involved Mosby's Rangers. A series of granite markers scattered throughout the county pays tribute to various engagements between Federal and Confederate forces. Erected in the 1890s by the J.E.B. Stuart Chapter of the Confederate Veterans, many of these markers memorialize small fights that have gone unrecognized in most history books, playing an important role in the preservation of local history. Two markers commemorate major engagements: the Battle of Cool Spring, near Castleman's Ferry, and the Battle of Berryville. Other memorialized engagements include: the Fight at Gold's Farm, in which Mosby's Rangers ambushed a Union force prior to the Battle of Berryville; the Buckmarsh Fight, also called the Great Wagon Train Raid; the Fight at Berry's Ferry, close to the present-day U.S. 50 bridge; the Fight at Double Tollgate, where the iconic Dinosaur Land now stands; the Vineyard Fight and the Mount Carmel Fight, both near Millwood; the Fight at Mount Airy at the intersection of Route 7 and Route 601; lastly, "No Prisoners" is engraved in granite at the intersection of Parshall Road and Hill and Dale Farm Lane, marking the location where Union soldiers in the act of burning Colonel Morgan's house were attacked by a contingent of Mosby's men.

With its role in the Civil War, it is only fitting that Clarke County is plagued by haunts from the bloodshed to this very day. There are reports of spectral soldiers crossing the river; late at night, the wounded moan in old buildings that once served as hospitals; witnesses see ghostly troops throughout the county. In one account, a second-shift worker claimed to regularly see a Confederate soldier run across the road near Millwood on his drive to work.

Introduction

Members of the Forty-Third Battalion, Virginia Cavalry, better known as Mosby's Rangers, pose for a group photograph with their leader. *From the Library of Congress Civil War Photographs, 1861–1865.*

An engraved granite slab marks a skirmish between Mosby's Rangers and a group of General Custer's troops who were burning a home. Outraged, Mosby's men killed thirty Union soldiers and refused to take prisoners. *Courtesy of the author.*

Introduction

After the Civil War ended, newly freed African Americans established a community on the outskirts of Berryville. Named Josephine City, after Josephine Williams, a former slave who purchased two lots from Ellen McCormick of Clermont Farm, the community was self-sufficient, with a school, grocery store, gas station, boardinghouse, restaurant, cemetery and churches.

Today, Josephine City lies within the limits of the town of Berryville and is part of the Josephine City Historical District. The National Register of Historic Places added the Josephine City Historical District to its registry in 2015.

Clarke County has long been a getaway destination for Washingtonians, Baltimoreans and those from the surrounding suburbs. The Crow's Nest, a historic home in Berryville, operated as a boardinghouse in the early 1900s and attracted Washingtonians hoping to escape the heat of the city during the summer. While the weather in the Shenandoah Valley is typical of the mid-Atlantic, with hot and humid summer temperatures, daytime temperatures are a few degrees cooler than in Washington, D.C., and the nights are considerably cooler. Before air conditioners were commonplace,

This historical marker commemorates Josephine City, an African American community established in the 1870s. The marker stands near the entrance of Josephine Street in Berryville. *Courtesy of the author.*

Introduction

homes west of the Blue Ridge were much more comfortable in the summer months than those to the east.

Today, Clarke County is still attracting visitors from the Baltimore and Washington, D.C. metro areas as a getaway. Outdoor enthusiasts flock to the county to hike the Appalachian Trail and for fishing, canoeing, kayaking and tubing on the Shenandoah River. Others enjoy weekend trips to pick fruit in the county's vast orchards, wine tasting at several vineyards, shopping at local farmer's markets or searching for valuable one-of-a-kind antiques.

This book explores hauntings, ghosts and paranormal activity in the county. Some are under the mistaken impression that Civil War ghosts and, to a lesser degree, colonial-era spirits are all that roam the area. Nothing could be further from the truth. While historic haunts are plentiful, there are also hauntings from the present day. A plane crashed into Mount Weather, leaving restless spirits behind to sift through the wreckage; malevolent entities roam the grounds of an abandoned church; an odd monster lets out bloodcurdling screams late at night along a back road that parallels the river; there are haunted woods and cemeteries; and newly constructed homes harbor ghosts. Perhaps unrelated, but strange nonetheless, Clarke County has had its share of UFO sightings and Bigfoot reports. All of this just barely scratches the surface.

Area folklore and traditions, local history and eyewitness accounts of paranormal activity come together in this book to bring the very best ghost stories to the reader. Dozens of witnesses were interviewed to provide a clear and accurate picture of the hauntings of Clarke County. In some cases, names were omitted to protect the anonymity of witnesses who wished to do so. In a few instances, specific locations have been withheld to ensure the privacy of those who have been gracious enough to come forward with their stories.

1
A DOOMED FLIGHT

That their mother, their wife, their son, daughter, lover died in a plane crash was, admittedly different. Not like a wreck on the highway or cancer, or even combat. A plane crash, because somehow public, becomes a happening, like murder on a crowded avenue. Yet, regardless of how they died, for those left behind, the gut-tearing emptiness, the mute three-in-the-morning despair is the same—an intimation of their own mortality.
—*Adam Shaw,* Sound of Impact: The Legacy of TWA Flight 514

Most anyone who lives within a thirty-mile radius of the Mount Weather Emergency Operations Center, better known as Mount Weather, operated by the Federal Emergency Management Agency (FEMA), has heard a teenage boy tell a story such as this: "My friend knows this guy who climbed the fence at Mount Weather and right after he did, all these guys in black ninja suits with submachine guns came repelling out of the trees and arrested him!"

Others have heard another popular variation of the tale: A paramilitary tactical unit apprehended the trespassers after they sneaked onto the federal land while deer hunting.

Then there are the stories of those accosted while riding dirt bikes or four-wheelers too close to the fence. Similar tales are told at bars, watercoolers, breakrooms, jobsites and wherever people like to spin yarns and speculate about what actually takes place at top-secret government installations. The internet is a lively source; chatrooms and message boards are hotbeds for these tall tales. From the outlandish to the plausible, stories about Mount Weather run the gamut, but the classified facility—complete with a subterranean city and state-of-the-art aboveground facilities—isn't giving up any of its secrets.

Mount Weather is a large employer of Clarke County residents; those who work there are very tight-lipped about the mysterious facility and the duties that they perform on-site. No one is hired to work at Mount Weather without first passing a complete background check and signing a nondisclosure agreement.

Nestled in the Blue Ridge Mountains, Mount Weather straddles both Loudoun and Clarke Counties and lies along State Route 601, which connects State Route 7 with U.S. 50. What is known about Mount Weather is that it is an integral part of the Continuity of Operations (COOP) plan of the federal government. COOP is an initiative to ensure that agencies can continue operations during times of crisis. Mount Weather, among other things, serves as a relocation site for high-ranking government officials during a state of emergency. For instance, when the infamous terrorist attacks took place on September 11, 2001, Vice President Dick Cheney was rushed to Mount Weather. More recently, the Department of Homeland Security issued a statement confirming that the site was briefly activated in April 2015 after major widespread power outages swept through Washington, D.C.

Rumors about Mount Weather and FEMA swirl around the internet. Secrecy has a way of breeding wild speculation. There is, however, a rumor that has at least an air of believability. According to some, there is a secret underground train system that runs from Washington, D.C., to Mount Weather. Others have said that this underground network expands much farther, perhaps even to Pennsylvania. Mount Pony, in Culpeper, Virginia, the former site of a Federal Reserve doomsday-style bunker, was also connected to Washington via secret rail, according to rumors. Whether or not these clandestine rail systems exist, secretive government "off sites" do; there are detailed plans and infrastructure in place to move essential government operations at a moment's notice. The federal government has specialized vehicles in its possession for these purposes, and it has a variety of designated off sites in Virginia, West Virginia, Maryland, Pennsylvania and beyond.

Curiously, there have been at least five documented unidentified flying objects (UFOs) spotted in Clarke County in recent memory. The sightings are logged into the databases of two UFO reporting groups, the Mutual UFO Network (MUFON), which has two reports, and the National UFO Reporting Center (NUFORC), which has three reports. There have been many other sightings from nearby locales such as Winchester, Stephens City, Front Royal and several towns across the mountain in Loudoun County. Sightings of UFOs regularly happen around military bases, secret government installations, hydroelectric dams, nuclear power plants and other facilities that are key to the security and infrastructure of the United States. It is fair to wonder: Could UFOs be patrolling the skies to keep an eye on places like Mount Weather?

Fans of the *X-Files* might recall "The Truth," a two-part episode that aired in 2002. In the episode, Agent Fox Mulder infiltrated Mount Weather with the help of the shadowy "Cigarette Smoking Man." Once inside, Mulder was able to gain access to the secure, highly secret computer system and learned of an impending alien invasion and colonization of earth. The date was set for December 22, 2012—one day after the last day recorded on the Mayan calendar!

TWA Flight 514

Today, Mount Weather and its location are known to many. Some things, but very little of substance, are known about its purpose—or, at least, its officially stated purpose. There was a time, however, when Mount Weather was virtually unknown to the public. This came to an end when a plane crashed into the mountain on Sunday, December 1, 1974.

As the nation was settling into its typical Sunday football ritual, a news bulletin flashed across the screen alerting viewers that a plane had slammed into a mountaintop about thirty miles from Dulles International Airport. The accident involved a Boeing 727, operated by the now defunct Trans World Airlines, with eighty-five passengers and seven crew members aboard. There were no survivors.

High crosswinds gusting up to fifty-six miles per hour made landing unsafe for Flight 514, whose original destination was Washington National Airport (now Reagan National Airport) in Washington, D.C. The flight was diverted to Dulles International Airport in Loudoun County, Virginia.

Trouble began with confusion over whether the plane was on a radar-controlled approach segment. (Fortunately, the clarification of language came about because of the tragedy.) The plane began a descent to 1,800 feet, and on reaching this altitude, deviations of up to 200 feet took place as fog and heavy snow affected visibility. At an altitude of 1,670 feet, the airliner slammed into the western slope of Mount Weather. The doomed aircraft sheared off treetops and, after crossing Route 601, crashed into a rocky outcrop. The plane disintegrated on impact, strewing fiery wreckage—and victims—over an area of about two hundred yards. Adam Shaw described the final moments of the ill-fated airliner and those onboard in his 1977 book *Sound of Impact*:

> *At 198 knots the screaming jet, left wing slightly dipped, hits the first black oak poking seventy feet up through the mist of Weather Mountain. It is 11:09:22 am. Within the next fraction of a second, like a giant lawn mower out of the sky, the plane cut a 380-foot swath through pine, spruce and oak, ripping and tearing its way lower and lower toward Route 601.*
>
> *The men in the cockpit were already dead—speared by the tree limbs shattering through the windshield. The jet crossed the road at fifteen feet, sinking. Nose-first, it bludgeoned into a basalt ledge on the far side of Route 601 and, quite simply, ceased to exist. A bloody rain of limbs and debris rose and then fell through the bare branches. Fires spread on the rock, on the soggy forest loam.*
>
> *The fog and the silence rolled back in.*

The scene was horrific—the stuff of nightmares. After seeing the carnage from the disaster, Bill Peters, a rescue worker from Sterling Park, described the macabre scene: "There were pieces all over the mountain, and they weren't very big pieces."

The force of the crash had ripped both clothing and limbs from the victims' bodies. Oliver Dube, the Loudoun County fire marshal, recalled, "I don't remember seeing any with shoes on." He went on. "There were pieces of arms and legs wrapped around trees. I saw one leg embedded in a tree."

Dr. George Hocker, the Loudoun County medical examiner, instructed rescue workers to try to keep pieces of bodies together. He later said to the press, "The rain has a way of cleaning bodies up, but you get the impression that someone had put all these people in a bag and just shook them out."

In the nearby Bluemont Community House, Dr. Hocker established a makeshift morgue. He ordered the windows opened and the heat cut to the building. Here, the grim work of identifying the dead would be carried out.

Ninety-two dead. Truly, a disaster of epic proportions had taken place on top of Mount Weather. Not since the War Between the States had the area seen such bloodshed.

Lost in the tragic tale of TWA Flight 514 is a piece of history often overlooked. Another Boeing 727 had crashed on the same day about three hundred miles away. Northwest Airlines Flight 6231 was en route to Buffalo, New York, to pick up the players of the National Football League's Baltimore Colts franchise. Icy conditions led to a crash that killed all three crewmembers onboard. Thankfully, there were no passengers.

Back at Mount Weather, shortly after the disastrous plane crash, federal officials ordered local police to seal the area. Some even believed that the secret facility, about a mile and a half away from the crash site, hampered recovery efforts. The Government Services Administration, which ran Mount Weather at the time for the Office of Preparedness, denied the allegations. A spokesperson said, "We provided ropes, trucks and personnel to help in the rescue effort. And coffee."

Paranormal Activity

Today, much of the trauma that descended on Mount Weather more than four decades ago lives on in the form of unexplained activity. In the woods, where body parts were strewn across the forest floor and draped over the trees themselves, screams have been heard at night. Visitors have spotted apparitions around the crash site, and some have even taken anomalous photographs at the site. There are reports from people who claim that an invisible force pushed them while walking along the large rock formation

TWA Flight 514 crashed into this outcrop on December 1, 1974, killing all ninety-two persons onboard. *Courtesy of the author.*

on the side of Route 601. Electronic voice phenomena (EVP) recordings in which the names of crash victims were uttered have been captured on-site. Some visitors have reported an overwhelming smell of jet fuel near the crash site. Other strange phenomena include the detection of cold spots (severe, localized dips in temperature) and spikes in electromagnetic frequency (EMF)—both thought by many to be evidence of the presence of ghosts.

Not everyone agrees that strange activity is occurring on Mount Weather near the crash site. While many believe it might be the most haunted spot on all the Blue Ridge, Tim lived near the crash site for over six years and did not experience anything like what has been described.

A Campfire Tale

Typing "TWA haunted" into an internet search engine will quickly lead to the story of a ghostly pilot who tried to hitch a ride from a long-haul truck driver. It is a remarkable story that first appeared in 2006, the kind of tale often told over a campfire on a dark and moonless night. Is the story true? Sadly, there is no way to know.

The tale begins with a truck driver dropping off a load in Winchester around 2:00 a.m. on a cold December night in 2004. After the delivery, the driver headed east on Route 7 on his way to his next stop in Washington, D.C. The trucker reached the "top of the mountain," and at the intersection of Route 601 and Route 7, he pulled over to look at his maps.

According to the driver, at the intersection, he pulled into a gas station that was closed at that late hour. A gas station? This is where the story goes off the rails for many longtime area residents. This point, however, will be addressed in the paragraphs to follow. While looking at his maps, he was approached by a stranger wearing a flight crew uniform. The man climbed onto the step of the cab, and the driver rolled his window down. At once, he noticed a strong odor—the smell of kerosene—on the stranger.

"Could you give me a lift?" the mystery man asked the trucker. "I can pay you."

The stranger was wearing a hat that bore TWA insignia; he said that he needed to get to Dulles Airport to work a flight. The driver agreed to take him as far as the next open store. Once there, he could call a cab to take him the rest of the way to Dulles. The airline employee thanked him and, as he climbed down, muttered, "He said we could descend."

The stranger walked around the front of the truck and suddenly vanished into the cold night air.

After grabbing a flashlight and searching the area unsuccessfully for the mysterious stranger, the truck driver continued with his load to D.C. Along the way, he remembered that TWA had gone out of business a couple of years earlier. Once he returned home, he did some research into the defunct airline and learned that thirty years ago, Flight 514 crashed several miles up Route 601 from where the ghostly airline employee approached him.

A Fascinating Ghost Story: Could It Be True?

Of course, anyone who has lived in the area for any length of time knows that there is no gas station on the mountain. Nor has there ever been. The site of the ghostly encounter serves as a commuter parking lot, and on the weekends, hikers from around the region park their cars there and set off for the Appalachian Trail. With this in mind, was the long-haul trucker simply spinning a yarn?

Before the lot in question became a commuter parking lot, the Virginia Department of Transportation (VDOT) used it for the storage of salt for times of inclement weather. Some older area residents may remember seeing salt storage facilities in the 1970s and 1980s. What is interesting, though, is that VDOT maintained fuel pumps for its trucks on the site until the mid- to late 1980s. Two longtime VDOT employees, one of whom was interviewed for this book, confirmed this.

Knowing that there were once gas pumps on the lot, could this have been what the trucker was referring to? Is it possible that the truck driver briefly slipped back in time on that night? Did he unaware step thirty years into the past? If so, could he have mistaken this lot, with its gas pumps, for a small gas station that was closed so late at night? Or, is this tale just one more in a long line of make-believe ghost stories? I have reached out to the storyteller several times in hopes of getting some clarification on the gas station, to no avail.

To this day, the earth still yields up pieces of crash debris from time to time—a grim reminder of the horrific accident that occurred so many years ago. Pieces of plastic, metal, cloth and cable occasionally make their way to the surface, revealing that something terrible happened here on a scale that is unimaginable—something that time cannot bury. Stories that may or may not be true aside, a drive up to the crash site on a moonless night is certain to give most anyone the chills. It is possible to see a ghost; many have. One might see an orb or hear a scream. Or the air may become heavy with the smell of fuel. Even if nothing strange were to happen, the sheer magnitude of the crash—ninety-two persons torn to pieces, their lives cut short—is deeply disturbing and haunting to the soul.

2
Haunted Backroads

Being a lightly populated and rural county, Clarke has more than its share of two-lane country roads. In and of itself, this is not all that unusual. What is unusual, however, is that a county so small in land area would have several roads that may be haunted. Among these are Crums Church Road, which has had its share of strange activity over the years, and Ebenezer Road, home to a haunted church and cemetery. Then there are two roads with sections of haunted woods along their sides; the first is in Webbtown, and the other is in Stringtown. In both locations, a person supposedly died by hanging, and at both sites, there is a long history of strange and frightening activity.

Wickliffe Road

A patch of woods lies along Wickliffe Road near the intersection of Cannon Ball Road in which many unsettling encounters have occurred throughout the years. Witnesses tell of hearing what they describe as the eerie sound of piano music emanating from the woods. A "typical" experience happens something like this: around midnight, the lightning bugs immediately stop flashing; a stiff breeze blows through the trees; then, the faint yet haunting low tones of a piano inexplicably fill the night air. As chilling as it may be to suddenly see the flicker of the lightning bugs go dark and to hear the piano play, if an encounter with the supernatural is going to take place in Betsy Murphy's Woods, this is the best possible outcome. There are worse things that happen in this eerie, wooded lot—things that are utterly terrifying.

A man who used to work in Webbtown near the woods claimed to have heard screaming take place nearby. He wondered if perhaps there might be something to the rumors of someone dying in the woods from a hanging. The answer is yes.

Legend holds that, long ago, as the clock struck midnight, a rejected and heartbroken Betsy Murphy hanged herself. Before taking her own life, she cursed the family of the man who rejected her. She claimed that she would take on the form of a turkey and haunt the woods until the last member of the family was dead. Apparently, the family of the man who broke Betsy's heart is alive and well today; she has yet to stop haunting the forest.

The haunted woods have been notorious for generations. Generations of hunters have had problems getting their dogs to hunt there. Witnesses have reported hearing screams coming from the woods; sometimes, the screams sound like a turkey. Carolyn Thompson recounted: "My father-in-law hunted back in the day in the woods where Betsy Murphy was. He always said she would holler and sound like a turkey."

Carolyn and her family used to live in an old farmhouse near Betsy Murphy's Woods. Two of her children had a strange encounter in which they saw an old lady in the house dressed in nineteenth-century clothing. "It scared the tar out of them," Carolyn said.

What could be lurking in this wooded area? This is hard to say. But, if dogs are afraid to hunt in these woods, it is probably best for people to avoid them, too!

Stringtown Road

The small, unincorporated community of Stringtown was established in the nineteenth century. Local historians believe its name is derived from the old idiom "living on a shoestring," as there was once a county poorhouse nearby. Heading toward Winchester from Route 7, Stringtown is reached by turning onto Kimble Road, just west of Berryville. For reasons unknown to the author, many longtime county residents call Kimble Road "Piece and Plenty." Once "turning down Piece and Plenty," the next road on the right is Stringtown Road. A patch of haunted woods lies along this two-lane country road. According to several folks raised nearby, the woods were even more eerie back in the 1980s and 1990s, before so many houses were built along the road to accommodate area growth.

It is easy for a driver to know when he or she has reached the haunted woods; there are two distinctive landmarks that give it away. First, there is a sharp bend in the road; second, there is a long, stout branch, about twenty feet off the ground, that stretches all the way across the road. The large tree branch that spans the road has been the site of much strange activity over the years. Passersby, driving late at night, have spotted someone hanging from the branch, only to turn around and see nothing.

Nicole and Kathleen, college students at James Madison University, were visiting for the weekend and drove down Stringtown Road. Nicole, well versed in the area's ghost lore, told Kathleen, who is from Pennsylvania, the tales of motorists who have spotted a ghostly victim dangling above the road. Once the pair reached the sharp turn, Kathleen immediately knew the spot of the phantom hangings—the branch is that distinctive! They did not observe anything strange themselves but remarked that there is an unmistakable "feel" that is tough to explain.

This ominous and easily recognizable tree branch spans Stringtown Road. *Courtesy of the author.*

Others agree with Nicole and Kathleen's assessment—even without seeing a spectral victim dangling from the tree limb, driving underneath it, particularly at night, creates an ominous feeling. Is it possible that the old poorhouse left some sort of negative energy behind that is felt to this day?

Ebenezer Road

A short distance, by the way the crow flies, from the TWA 514 crash site covered in the first chapter, is Ebenezer Road. This road is reached from Route 7 East and lies about halfway up the mountain before reaching the Loudoun County line. It is a heavily wooded, winding road with several sharp turns; the two-lane road rises and falls as it follows the contour of hills, reaching several crests before dropping sharply and climbing again.

It might be a bit of a mischaracterization to call Ebenezer Road haunted, although driving the road late at night can feel a bit spooky. It is not the road itself that deserves attention, but rather an old dilapidated church that lies alongside it. This abandoned church might be one of the scariest places in all of Clarke County. From its outward appearance, Ebenezer Church looks like any one of thousands of small, old country churches that have outlived their time. But here, the old adage holds true—looks can be deceiving.

Ebenezer Church sits on a hill about one hundred yards from the road. During the summer months, when the trees are in full foliage, the church is easy to miss; it is barely visible, and a driver can pass right by without noticing it. Those familiar with the church, or first-time visitors who happen to notice the church's unwelcoming entrance, will drive up a narrow, rutted and washed-out gravel driveway that leads to a small parking area in front of the main entrance of the church. Though the parking area is small, it is hard to imagine a time when the church would have needed more parking space.

The small white church is in desperate need of a paint job. The chalky paint is peeling off the wood siding and the trim, much of which has rotted and is in dire need of replacement. The mud daubers have staked their claim on the church, their nests filling the spacing where the siding overlaps; hornet nests line the roof overhang like Christmas ornaments. A church bell at the front entrance has a broken rope; clearly, no one has rung the bell in ages. The doors to the church are closed tight and padlocked; the windows have long been boarded up. Beside the church is a picnic shelter nearly as large as the church itself. One can't help but wonder how often the space is used.

The small, abandoned Ebenezer Church and adjacent cemetery have a long history of hauntings. *Courtesy of the author.*

Ebenezer Church gives the impression that its cemetery, not the worship house, is the main attraction. A canopy of hardwood trees covers the largest area of the cemetery, and weeds and underbrush suffocate many of the gravestones along the edge of the property. Despite the ill-kept graves along the perimeter, many of the tombstones on-site are neat and tidy, with recently placed flowers and American flags. The layout of the cemetery is peculiar and lacks any sort of cohesion. There are small areas surrounded by a chain; extremely old headstones are intermingled with fairly recent ones; graves throughout the cemetery lay vertically, horizontally and even diagonally. The haphazard placement of the graves seems a little odd.

There are a handful of unmarked graves in the cemetery and a few marked only by rocks. These were probably poor people whose surviving family members could not afford an engraved headstone. Many of the older gravestones are so badly weathered that the inscriptions are nearly illegible. Several infants and young children are laid to rest in the cemetery—always a heart-wrenching thing to see.

It is tough to explain, but many who visit Ebenezer Church mention a sense of uneasiness that they cannot shake while they are there. This feeling often comes to daytime visitors—fright and panic can overtake those who tread the grounds at night.

"Way back when I used to drive a truck for VDOT, I used to have to go up there and plow snow," said a former Virginia Department of Transportation employee. "I used to hate going up by that place."

A former county deputy was not a big fan of Ebenezer Church, either. He said, "I used to hate going up there in the middle of the night."

Many middle-aged folks who grew up in Clarke County will probably remember Ebenezer Church as a party spot in the 1980s and early 1990s. A partygoer recounted an instance at the church that scared her so badly she never went back. This, of course, took place "back in the day" when the church doors were always open—before heavy padlocks and boarded windows barred the entrance of meddlesome youths. "One night, we were up there partying when I was about fifteen," she said. "We went into the old church to check it out, and I'm not kidding—when we left, both of those old church doors slammed shut!" This frightened all of the kids, and they could not leave quick enough. "I remember running through the little graveyard getting back to the car," she said. "I never went back there."

Another woman who used to go to Ebenezer Church in the late 1980s and early 1990s with her friends said, "We used to go up there and party. I just went because everybody else did; I thought it was scary." She continued: "Back in those days, you could go up there and the church was always open. There was a dare back then to see who could stay inside the church the longest without a flashlight with the doors shut." She went on to tell of kids who would go running out of the church screaming. As a joke, sometimes their friends outside the church would hold the doors shut, blocking the exit of the terrified thrill seekers. "I think all those times I went up there is why I won't set foot in a haunted house during the Halloween season," she said. "That place scared me half to death."

A college student recalled a visit to Ebenezer Church while he was home for a break. He and a friend drove to the church late at night and walked the perimeter of the building.

"It was cold and silent," he said. "I got an eerie feeling about the place."

The pair took a series of pictures with their iPhones in hopes that something anomalous would show up in at least one of the photographs, but it was not to be. Even after downloading the pictures onto a laptop and looking at them on the larger screen, there was nothing odd about any of the photographs.

The pictures were a bit of a disappointment, but the young men did observe electromagnetic frequency fluctuations toward the back of the church building using an EMF meter.

"Walking in the graveyard, it felt like I was being watched," said the witness. And apparently, he no longer has a burning curiosity about Ebenezer Church. He said, "It's fair to say I don't need to go back there again."

Jeannie Marie Combs is a local resident who grew up in Pine Grove; she has many family members buried in the cemetery, and she visits often. When asked why Ebenezer Church seems to have such a high concentration of strange activity—up to and including malevolent entities roaming the grounds—she said there is a portal of some sort on-site. If this is the case, it might explain why visitors often report malevolent spirits wandering the cemetery, woods and church building. These entities are crossing through to this side at the same time and in the same way as neutral and benevolent entities do. Think of a giant and invisible doorway into a realm that we cannot see. Jeannie claims to have photographed hundreds of multicolored orbs on-site. This would seem to indicate that something is indeed rushing through this theoretical doorway.

Jeannie warns those with a negative aura not to visit Ebenezer Church. This is probably good advice. People who play around with the unknown, especially out of morbid curiosity, often end up with a lot more than they bargained for.

CRUMS CHURCH ROAD

Crums Church Road lies just west of Berryville and connects Harry Byrd Highway, or Route 7, with Old Charlestown Road. Many strange things occur along this two-lane country road. To a paranormal enthusiast, this should come as no surprise given the Civil War history of the area. When farmers plow their fields and homeowners till their gardens that lie along the road, they often find spent musket balls, buttons and other items from the war.

At the intersection of Old Charlestown Road, there is a small historic church known as Stone's Chapel. Built in 1848 and named after Jacob Stone, the brick chapel replaced an eighteenth-century log structure. Adjacent to the chapel lies a small cemetery that holds dozens of weathered and leaning headstones, many of which have been in place for more than two hundred years. Many of the inscriptions on the headstones are completely illegible due to excessive weathering. The cemetery serves as the final resting place for veterans from both the Revolutionary War and the War Between the States.

The headstone of a Confederate veteran who served under the command of the "Gray Ghost," Colonel John Singleton Mosby. *Courtesy of the author.*

Veterans from both the Revolutionary War and the Civil War are laid to rest at the Stone's Chapel Cemetery. This is the grave of one such veteran. *Courtesy of the author.*

Stone's Chapel is no stranger to weird activity; it has a history of a light that randomly turns itself on. Of course, a skeptic could explain this in any number of ways, including faulty wiring; however, people have seen the light shining in the church during a period of extended vacancy in which the building had no power! There have been strange occurrences in the cemetery, too. Inexplicable pockets of cold air and a sensation of "unexplainable static electricity" have taken place. Additionally, visitors to the grounds have photographed orbs at night. Understandably, many are skeptical of orbs. Typically, dust, insects or water droplets that cannot be seen by the photographer cause orbs—glowing, colored balls of light—to appear in photographs. However, in areas known for paranormal activity, photographers often capture orbs on camera—sometimes in large numbers—leading many to think that they might be some sort of manifestation of supernatural energy.

Leaving the chapel behind, a story comes from a lady who lived in an old farmhouse along Crums Church Road. In something that resembles a modern-day horror movie, she believed three malevolent entities were present in the house. These evil spirits would often attack her and her

The historic Stone's Chapel and Cemetery sits at the intersection of Crums Church Road and Old Charles Town Road. *Courtesy of the author.*

daughters. The earthly occupants of the home suffered through bouts of hair-pulling and other attacks. An unseen force even pushed the mother down a flight of stairs!

Carla Kay White-Welch tells of a friendly spirit that lives in her home, which lies along Crums Church Road. The house stands on the spot where a log cabin was built in the 1780s. Referred to locally as the "White House," due to the many generations of Whites who have lived there, the home's nickname is quite fitting. Carla and her family had long suspected the presence of friendly spirits in her home; however, she would receive confirmation of this belief in a most shocking way.

One day, Carla walked down the stairs to find her four-year-old nephew talking to himself, as children do. The boy was in a deep and serious conversation, much more so than normal.

"Who are you talking to?" Carla asked jokingly.

"Your ghost," replied the young boy.

"Oh really?" she responded. "Well, what is this friendly ghost's name, Casper?"

"No, it's Soley," her nephew relied. "He said you would remember his straw hat."

It so happens that Soley was Carla's grandmother's brother-in-law. She remembered that Soley stayed with the family for a while after his wife passed away. When Carla was about five or six years old, Soley passed away. She has very little recollection of the man, except for one thing: his straw hat!

Carla also recalls a story from her youth in which she learned of paranormal activity taking place in a farmhouse about half a mile from where she lives. One day, as a teenager, she went with her mother to an estate auction. She remembered that her mother was shocked that someone would want to sell such a nice piece of property. The owner, however, saw things much differently. "The owner told us he couldn't wait to get it off his hands," Carla said.

The homeowner went on to share with Carla and her mother that he had been experiencing ghostly activity in the house. After conducting some research, he learned that his home once served as an unofficial, makeshift hospital during the Civil War. At night, he would often hear the moans and cries of wounded soldiers along with the murmuring of the medical staff. He also saw horses in his barn outfitted with gear of the Confederate States of America. In and of itself, this might not have been enough to force the man out of his estate, which featured a barn, outbuildings and a beautiful home sitting on a vast parcel of prime land. However, as things often do where paranormal activity is concerned, things would get worse for the homeowner—much worse.

The man went on to recount the story of his Oriental rug—a large and expensive Oriental rug—that was in one of the rooms in his house. He noticed that it had developed an odd rust-colored stain. So, one day, he removed the rug and dropped it off with the cleaners. While the rug was gone, he noticed that the stain went all the way down to the wood floor. One night, he noticed that where the rug used to lie, the floor was wet and there was a thick, sticky substance present. Perplexed, the man reached down and sniffed the goo—the unmistakable smell of blood filled his nostrils. As hard as the distraught man tried, he could not get his floor clean; the substance kept oozing out. The next morning, however, the puddle of blood was gone and the floor was dry, but the rusty stain remained. Over a series of several nights, the man observed the stain. He found that the blood would appear around 11:00 p.m., and by about 6:00 a.m., it was gone. Sometime later, he learned that this room once served as an amputation room during the war. Apparently, each night, phantom surgeons were amputating ghostly limbs. Over a century after the war ended, this was still taking place inside his home!

The final straw for the troubled homeowner came when he opened his journal one morning. He sat down to make an entry, the same as any morning, and turned in the book to what should have been the next blank page. The page, however, was not blank; there was a note written in ink from an old quill pen. It read:

I just need to find my leg! If I don't, I'll take yours!
—HB

With this, the property went up for auction almost immediately.

3
Historic Haunts of Berryville

The small town of Berryville is the seat of Clarke County. According to numbers obtained in 2016, the population stands at just above 4,300 residents. Its size should not fool you; Berryville has a history that rivals towns that are much larger.

Under the employment of Lord Fairfax, George Washington, a teenager at the time, surveyed Berryville in 1750. Washington's adopted granddaughter, Eleanor "Nellie" Custis Lewis, moved to the Audely Plantation, on the outskirts of Berryville, around 1830.

Daniel Morgan, a hero of the American Revolution nicknamed the "Old Wagoner," took up residence in Berryville at the historic farmhouse known as Soldier's Rest for a time after the war. According to former residents, Soldier's Rest, built around 1780, was constructed with a series of secret passages underneath the house. Morgan went on to build a home near Boyce that he named Saratoga in honor of his participation in the Battles of Saratoga—the turning point in the war in favor of the American forces. Morgan died on his sixty-sixth birthday at his daughter's house on Amherst Street in Winchester. His daughter's former home, which is privately owned, is quite haunted, according to local rumor.

As a young man, the scrappy Morgan would engage in fights with local ruffians at the intersection of Winchester Turnpike and Charlestown Road. As the stories go, Morgan kept piles of rocks stashed nearby in case he needed them during his many altercations.

In Berryville's early days, the small community earned itself the nickname "Battletown." In their 1940 book *Legends of the Skyline Drive and the Great Valley of Virginia*, authors Carrie Hunter Willis and Etta Belle Walker said:

> *Long before the County of Clarke was ordered to be carved from Frederick, a town was established called Battletown. This was so called, says tradition, because of the rough-and-tumble fights of the gang who met there to drink their ale.*
>
> *Daniel Morgan, a picturesque character of the valley, thought he had the right to stop such fights and frequently got into the fray. Old records show that Morgan sometimes had to pay a fine "for misbehavior." But no doubt it was here that he won his strength and learned to outmatch the toughs of the neighborhood. Certainly, he won a reputation for his prowess, and as a general he won distinction.*

In 1798, the Virginia General Assembly granted the request of Benjamin Berry to establish a town. Battletown became officially known as Berryville. Benjamin Berry built one of the town's most famous landmarks, the Battletown Inn.

This historic marker in Berryville pays tribute to town founder Benjamin Berry. *Courtesy of the author.*

The Shenandoah Valley was known as "The Granary" and "The Bread Basket of the Confederacy" during the War Between the States. The entire valley became a hotly contested battleground, and the small town of Berryville saw its share of activity during the conflict. Confederate lieutenant general Jubal Early's headquarters was in Berryville for a short time during the war. While on his way to Gettysburg, General Robert E. Lee made a stop in Berryville to camp. In September 1864, the Battle of Berryville, a conflict that ended without a clear victor, resulted in over six hundred combined casualties and losses.

Mosby's Raiders attacked General Philip Sheridan's supply train just outside of town on August 13, 1864. The daring raid resulted in quite a bounty for the partisan rangers. The raiders seized two hundred head of cattle and made off with more than six hundred mules and horses. In addition, two hundred prisoners were apprehended. The raid also scored one hundred supply wagons. During the raid, Mosby's men chased some Union soldiers into town. The soldiers sought refuge in the Berryville Baptist Church, located east of the present church cemetery.

Several of Mosby's cavalrymen rode into the building firing their weapons, which did great damage to the church. Bullet holes remained in the walls long after the altercation. Congregants erected the present Berryville Baptist Church on the other side of the cemetery in 1884. They outfitted the new church with a magnificent set of spiral staircases, the only of their kind in the area. The staircases would surely prevent any future cavalrymen from charging up the steps on horseback. This was the Lord's house, after all!

With a legacy that stretches back to colonial times, it should come as no surprise that Berryville has more than its share of haunted history, much of which lives on in its many historic homes.

Haunted Historic Homes

Major Charles Smith was an early resident of Berryville. He served under Lieutenant Colonel George Washington at Fort Necessity in 1754. A few years later, Washington chose Smith to oversee the construction of Fort Loudoun in Winchester. Washington designed the fort as part of defensive measures taking place on the frontier during the French and Indian War. Washington liked and trusted Smith and would go on to hire him as his personal accountant.

Smith had a brush with the law in 1757 after he killed a man with one punch at a tavern in Fredericksburg, Virginia. The *Maryland Gazette* of Annapolis reported the following on September 22, 1757:

> *Last Thursday an unhappy Affair happened at Fredericksburg in Virginia: Thomas Frazier, our late faithful diligent Post-Rider, getting in some Dispute in a Tavern with an Officer of the Virginia Regiment, the Officer gave him a Blow with his Hand in the Face, of which he died in about Three Quarters of an Hour. The Officer immediately delivered himself to the Justice, and ordered a decent Burial for the Deceased.*

The authorities cleared Smith of any wrongdoing in the death.

In 1765, Smith's father-in-law, Colonel John Hite, sold him a tract of land in what would become Berryville. Smith named his estate Battletown and built a house where a rowdy tavern once stood. The home, known as "The Nook," still stands today on East Main Street and has the distinction of being the oldest house in town.

Judi, a former resident of the home, believes with a certainty that it is haunted. During the four years she lived there, without giving specific examples, she claims that many strange things occurred in the house.

The Nook is thought to be the oldest home in Berryville. *Courtesy of the author.*

"Little Phil," Major General Philip Sheridan, who commanded the Union's Army of the Shenandoah, poses for a photograph outside his tent. *From the Library of Congress Civil War Photographs, 1861–1865.*

The Crow's Nest, occupied by General Philip Sheridan during the Valley campaigns of 1864, serves as an apartment building today. *Courtesy of the author.*

Others have mentioned strange sounds and electrical anomalies taking place in the home.

One could probably say those things about most any home in town whose construction occurred prior to the Civil War. Take the Crow's Nest, for instance, an antebellum home built in 1848 by Thomas Crow that has its share of strange activity. General Philip Sheridan took over the house several times during his Shenandoah Valley campaign and used it as his headquarters. In the attic was a secret room covered by a panel in the wall. Residents used the room to hide things of value when Federal forces occupied the town. Legend holds that Confederate soldiers who became trapped behind enemy lines when the Union took control of Berryville also hid in the well-concealed room.

Today, the Crow's Nest is as an apartment building. Former and current residents alike have reported strange activity in the building. Most notably, the apparitions of a Confederate soldier and a woman dressed in Civil War–era clothing have made appearances in the old house. Are the soldier and the woman by-products of the war, energy left behind in the form of apparitions? Could this lady have hidden Confederate soldiers from the Yankees during the war? Is she still trying to keep them safe all these years after the war ended?

The Battletown Inn

If you decide to insult a southern man's honor, then you had better be prepared for a fistfight—maybe worse. This is every bit as true today as it was 150 years ago. Whatever the reason, southern men adhere to a "culture of honor," and they often meet insults and even perceived slights with aggression. Today, however, there are fewer formalities associated with defending one's honor than there were in the 1800s.

Long before Colonel John S. Mosby rode through Clarke County and vast swaths of the Virginia countryside as commander of the Forty-Third Battalion, Virginia Cavalry, he spent much of his youth defending his honor against bullies. The diminutive Mosby found himself an easy target. Early in life, he learned to defend himself, and he grew up to become a plucky young man, never one to back down from a challenge.

While enrolled in the University of Virginia, a well-known bully named George Turpin put Mosby's honor to the test. Turpin insulted Mosby, who, when learning of the slight, responded to Turpin with a letter. As strange as it sounds today, answering an insult by letter was a formality among southern men of the day. When Turpin read Mosby's letter, he became enraged and declared, "I'll eat him up raw!"

Prior to confronting Turpin, Mosby armed himself with a small pepperbox pistol—an equalizer against the enormous and athletically built Turpin. When the two met, Mosby faced Turpin and said, "I hear you've been making assertations." With this, Turpin charged Mosby. Physically, Mosby was no match for the hulking Turpin, so he pulled out his pepper-box pistol and fired a shot into his attacker's neck. Amazingly, and fortunately for both men, Turpin went on to recover from his wounds.

The authorities arrested Mosby for the incident, and the University of Virginia expelled him while he awaited trial. Mosby served a year in jail for the incident. The court ultimately found him guilty of the misdemeanor charge of an "unlawful shooting."

Mosby's actions demonstrate the extreme that a southern man of his day would go to to defend his sacred honor. But, what of a nineteenth-century southerner who had his honor stripped away without a way to correct things? What could an insulted and brokenhearted man do when confronting those who had wronged him was not an option? What could he do when there was simply no way to set things right again?

Many decades ago, these questions may have been answered at one of the most recognizable landmarks in Berryville, the Battletown Inn, located on West Main Street. The Battletown Inn served as a hospital during the War Between the States, and local legend holds that a wounded Confederate soldier fell in love with a nurse who cared for him. Though his wounds healed, his pain was only beginning. You see, he was forsaken by the love of his life—she ran off and married a Union soldier! Of all things for a Civil War–era southern man to bear, his lover ran off with a Federal soldier! It is one thing for a woman to choose another man in your stead—sometimes this happens in love. But to marry a Yankee? A Yankee! How could he go on without his love? How could she have insulted him so? How could he ever move on from such duplicity? The loss, pain and heartbreak, and the blow to his pride and insult to his honor were all too much for the man to bear. Completely crushed and having no way to restore his honor, the tormented loser in love hanged himself in the inn's former Gray Ghost Tavern.

Unfortunately for the brokenhearted soldier, he never truly escaped the pain of this world; his spirit still lingers, and visitors have felt his presence on

The historic and iconic Battletown Inn on West Main Street in Berryville is renowned for its hauntings. *Courtesy of the author.*

the second floor. Some say that he sits and looks out of a window, watching and waiting, hoping for the return of the woman who broke his heart.

The Battletown Inn might just be the most haunted location in town; even folks who are unacquainted with Clarke County's many ghostly tales have heard the stories from the inn. Perhaps the best accounts come from former employees such as Laura Rodgers. Laura worked at the inn in the late 1980s, and her supervisors would often assign her to work parties held upstairs. Late one night, while cleaning up after an event, she had an unforgettable encounter.

To help get through the arduous task of cleaning, the staff would play upbeat music, heard in any room of the house through a speaker system. "I was getting along cleaning, singing, and dancing and decided to take a big tray of dishes down the long flight of stairs," said Laura. "Just as I turned the corner, a lady with a beautiful white southern dress was turning the corner in the other room." The mysterious lady in the dress shot Laura an unfriendly glare and then vanished. Laura suspected the music must have upset the strange lady.

Laura knew that the ghostly woman had to have been from another time. She said, "No one looked or dressed that way." She wondered, "Was she a previous owner? Was she someone's love? Was she simply a guest?"

To this day, she has not been able to identify the mysterious woman in the dress.

Laura also tells of strange things that took place in the kitchen, but it was the basement of the inn, accessible from the front of the house, that was the spot of another bizarre and unforgettable experience.

"We always used the top landing of the basement stairs for storage of things like the broom and pan and the upright vacuum cleaner," recalled Laura. "Of course, my night to vacuum I go to get the upright and it wasn't there. I looked down the stairs and there it was. It toppled almost all the way down and some parts were on the dirt ground floor at the bottom."

Laura reluctantly went down into the basement to retrieve the vacuum cleaner. Immediately, she felt cold, and a wave of emotions swept over her. She said, "I felt sad, mad, and scared. I could feel that this is where people were, and this is where people died. I felt pain."

In her mind's eye, images flashed of soldiers lying against the stone walls and on the cold, dirt floor. There is little doubt that Laura caught a glimpse deep into the past, when the Battlefield Inn was a makeshift infirmary, used to house and treat those who suffered wounds during the war.

Rosemont

On the western edge of Berryville, sitting on sixty acres of some of the finest land in all of the Commonwealth of Virginia, is the historic and stately Rosemont Manor. Judge George Horton Norris, who would go on to become the first high sheriff of Clarke County, built the original home and named it Rose Mont in 1811 as a wedding present for his bride, Jane Bowles Wormeley.

Rosemont found its way into the hands of the Tyson family of Baltimore in the mid-nineteenth century, when Norris's granddaughter married into the family. In those days, the Tysons were known for two things: they were East Coast metal production tycoons, and they raised some of the nation's best racehorses. The Tyson family held on to Rosemont for fifty years, during which time they added what would become the favorite feature of many who visit the home: the grand portico.

In September 1864, Union forces lined both sides of Rosemont during the Battle of Berryville. Over the course of two days, the battle claimed 314 casualties among Federal forces, and the Confederacy suffered 295 casualties and losses. Many relics from the war have been recovered on the grounds of Rosemont over the years, but perhaps the best reminder of the conflict is the paranormal activity that occurs on the property.

The grand portico makes Rosemont one of the most beautiful homes in not only the Shenandoah Valley but also in all of Virginia. *Courtesy of the author.*

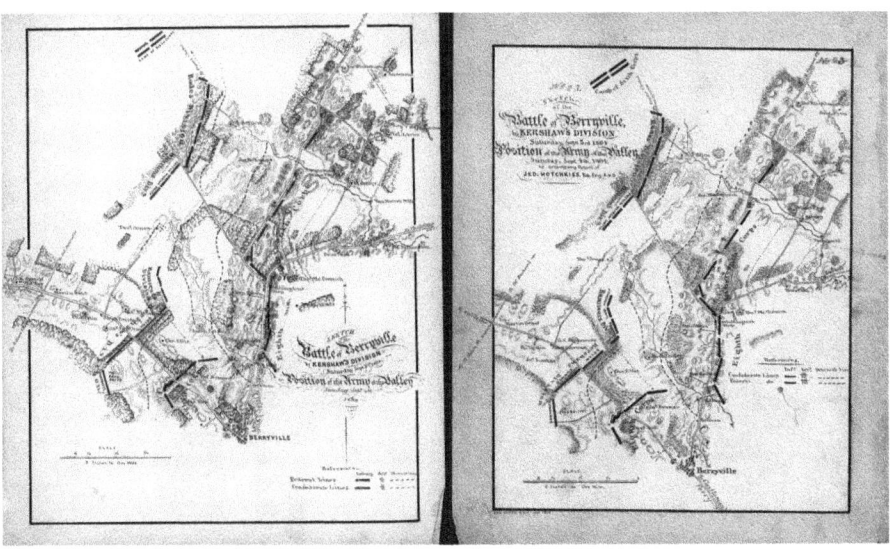

This map by Jedediah Hotchkiss shows Union and Confederate positions during the Battle of Berryville. *From the Library of Congress Geography and Map Division.*

An attorney from New York, J. Low Harriman, purchased Rosemont in 1910 and sold the estate seven years later. It was during Harriman's ownership that plumbing was added to the home.

Harry F. Byrd Sr., who served as the governor of Virginia and later represented the commonwealth for thirty-two years in the United States Senate, made Rosemont his home in 1929 and lived there until his death in 1966. Byrd was the architect and leader of the Byrd Organization, a political machine that dominated Virginia politics for decades. Byrd's home at Rosemont became a haven for politicians, and there was even a helicopter landing pad on the grounds, used for shuttling around high-ranking political figures.

Today, Rosemont operates as a bed-and-breakfast and hosts weddings and special events. It is also open during the Christmas season, and the entrance fees are donated to local nonprofits. Many of the rooms in the home take their names from historical icons who have stayed at Rosemont over the years. Some of these include Franklin Roosevelt, Dwight Eisenhower, John Kennedy, Richard Nixon, Lyndon Johnson, Charles Lindbergh, Albert Einstein and Admiral Chester W. Nimitz.

The Roosevelt Suite, once a billiard and game room under former owners, is where Harry F. Byrd Sr. passed away in 1966. In this room, a mischievous ghost once tried to keep a bride-to-be, also known as a "First Lady of Rosemont," awake on the night before her big day. According to the story, she was lying in bed, and the doors in the room began opening and slamming shut on their own. This continued for a while. When she finally had enough, she cried out, "You're going to stop! I'm getting married in the morning!" Fortunately, the spirit complied and allowed the bride to get her beauty rest.

"They'll play tricks," said Michael Haymaker, the director of weddings and design at Rosemont. "They will slam doors and lock doors or unlock doors and open doors."

The Kennedy Suite, on the upper level, is Matilda's bedroom—Matilda is Rosemont's most notable ghost. Matilda lived at Rosemont in the nineteenth century. A horse enthusiast who loved riding, Matilda suffered a tragic accident in the 1870s that left her bedridden and unable to care for herself. While riding one day, her horse fell, throwing her off, and her head smashed into a rock. After the accident, Matilda lived out her days in the Kennedy Suite, which was outfitted with a two-way mirror so that her caretaker in the adjacent room could better look after her.

Matilda is bedridden no longer; in fact, she has been seen floating dressed in her distinctive hooped skirt. No longer confined to her bed, Matilda

The Kennedy Suite is where Rosemont's most notable ghost, Matilda, lived out her days after she suffered a debilitating injury. *Courtesy of the author.*

The Roosevelt Suite at Rosemont once served as a game and billiards room under former owners. Today, many brides-to-be spend the night there before their big day. *Courtesy of the author.*

makes her way around the house; she leaves her room and goes down the steps and later returns. Sometimes, she pays Haymaker a visit in his office. The sweet smell of apples and apple blossoms often accompany Matilda—a dead giveaway that she is nearby.

The sweet smell that sometimes announces Matilda has entered the room commonly occurs in the paranormal world. This phenomenon takes place in the ballroom at the renowned Stanley Hotel in Estes Park, Colorado, made famous by films such as *The Shining* and *Dumb and Dumber*. Occasionally, Mrs. Stanley's perfume fills the air of the ballroom, making her presence known. In other paranormal locations, the scent of violets fills the air, indicating the presence of a spirit. Things aren't always so rosy with paranormal smells, however. It is just as common for foul odors—a noxious burning smell or the whiff of rotten eggs—to accompany spirits and even strange creatures.

Another commonality in the paranormal world is a phenomenon in which certain people are more in tune with the presence of spirits than others. While many folks can live in a house rumored to be haunted for many years and defiantly claim that nothing strange takes place there, people who are "sensitive" might walk into the very same house and have a paranormal encounter right away. A sensitive is simply someone who exhibits a heightened awareness of the paranormal and an ability to see or interact with things that most cannot.

A former Rosemont employee who was a sensitive used to see many young men walking in and out of a room. She did not say if they were in uniform or not, but it seems likely that they may have been. Many men were killed on the site during the War Between the States, and a number were buried on Rosemont property. During his ownership, Harry F. Byrd Sr. had many of the bodies exhumed and reinterred at the Arlington National Cemetery. With that said, there are still some fallen soldiers laid to rest on the grounds of Rosemont.

Apparitions "coming and going," especially around old battle sites, are typically thought of as residual hauntings. The best way to think of a residual haunting is to picture a scene from a movie playing on an endless loop. Whereas intelligent hauntings feature entities that interact with the living—they slam doors, move objects and do other such things—whatever is being seen in a residual haunting does not engage the living and may even seem oblivious to its surroundings. Some believe that rather than actual spirits, residual hauntings come from energy left behind at the location of a traumatic event. This residual energy plays out a scene from when the parties involved were alive, and this occurs decades and even centuries into the future.

The intelligent haunts of Rosemont have free run of the house. The attic is a hot spot for activity, as is the Nimitz Lounge and the Rosemont Room. These entities have a way of communicating and making their feelings known. Michael Haymaker said, "They'll let you know if they are happy or unhappy." For instance, a man sat in a chair, and this must not have gone over well with a resident spirit. Several of the younger people in his party were using a ghost-hunting app on their smartphones, and one of them detected an entity over the chair that said, "Get out of my chair!"

It wasn't until 2010 that Rosemont opened its doors to the public, thanks to owners William and Barbara Genda. Few antebellum homes can match the splendor of the house and its picturesque landscape. The ghosts, such as Matilda, make it all the more alluring.

4
THE COURTHOUSE GROUNDS

The Clarke County Courthouse on North Church Street is an easily recognizable landmark in the town of Berryville. It is also well known for its ghosts. Construction began on the courthouse shortly after the formation of the county in the late 1830s. Extensive remodeling occurred around 1850, and in 1882, the county built an office for the commonwealth's attorney on the courthouse grounds. In 1895, the sheriff's office and combination jail were built. Today, this building serves as a combination sheriff's office and 911 communications center. Bars still line the upstairs windows—a stark reminder that all manner of criminals were once held there.

While working in the courthouse during the 1980s, unexplained noises, moving objects and other strange activity plagued a janitor while he performed his duties each night. According to the former custodian, objects had the tendency to move on their own: "I would go to check, and chairs would be rearranged. I'd arrange them back and when I would come back later it was rearranged again." One room was worse than all the others. "There was one room in particular that was always rearranged. That room I would always save until last, so it wouldn't get rearranged by the time I left in the morning."

The former janitor has expressed sympathy for whoever cleans the building now. "The building was very scary."

Perhaps bad energy lingers in the area from all of the criminals that the county tried, confined and even hanged on the courthouse grounds. The

Left: Bars still line the windows of the old jail. *Courtesy of the author.*

Below: The Clarke County Courthouse is both historic and haunted. *Courtesy of the author.*

last hanging that took place on-site occurred in 1905. At ten o'clock on Friday morning, January 27, 1905, Benjamin C. Lippkin was hanged for the murder of Richard Ellerson. On July 7, 1904, Lippkin had shot the thirty-three-year-old Ellerson four times—twice in the back.

Before his execution, Lippkin claimed to have found redemption and salvation in Jesus Christ. He penned a letter to the citizens of Clarke County expressing regret for his actions while at the same time offering hope in Christ to others whose lives had gone astray. The letter appeared in the *Clarke Courier* in the Wednesday, January 18, 1905 issue. The paper described Lippkin as "a negro of considerable education…traveled around enough to absorb a great deal of information." Lippkin's letter, printed verbatim, reads:

> *To the public:*
> *I will say my time of departure is near at hand, but I am ready to be offered up and now am sweetly resting on the promise of God who is my*

Savior, and not only mine, but a Saviour to all who will come to him. Oh! could I known the salvation of the Lord Jesus Christ earlier, how much better and how much good I could have done to my fellowmen. But I thank God that he has remembered mercy instead of merit. The hymn that converted me was started by Mrs. Lizzie Jackson, who broke down and called to the Mrs. Lupton and some other white friends to assist her, which they willingly did. I thank my many friends, both white and colored, for the kindness they have contributed to me, and may God bless them all, for God has declared whosoever shall give drink unto one of these little ones a cup of cold water only in the name of his disciple shall in no wise lose his reward. I have nothing against the prosecutor or twelve jurors, and may God bless them all that I may meet them around the dazzling throne of God in the morning when the trumpet shall sound. They have only carried out the laws of this land. But had I not known sin I would not have committed the deed.

I wandered on in darkness:
Not a ray of light could I see;
And the thought filled my heart with sadness—
There's no hope for a sinner like me.

And then in that dark and lonely hour
A voice sweetly whispered to me,
Saying Christ, the Redeemer has power
To save a poor sinner like me.

I listened, and lo! 'twas the Savior
That was speaking so kindly to me:
I cried, "I am chief of sinners;
Thou cans't save a poor sinner like me."

My verse is this—

No longer in darkness I'm walking,
For the light is now shining on me;
And now unto others I'm telling
How He saved a poor sinner like me.

I am in peace with all mankind and when the hour comes to die I will step over the line in trust, and may God show his saving power to other sinful men and women in this land, and may my state be a warning to others who are traveling the road to ruin and seem to love their distance well. When this world's troubles are over I will go home to wear my crown.
—*Ben C. Lippkin*

In the same article that featured Lippkin's letter, the *Clarke Courier* went on to discuss details pertaining to the execution. For instance, Clarke County purchased the scaffolding for the hanging from neighboring Jefferson County, West Virginia. Discussed in the piece were other details, such as who would attend the execution:

The witnesses to the execution will be by card only, and it is believed the number will be as small as possible.

Regarding who shall be present at executions section 4063 of the Code of Virginia says: The Sheriff "shall be attended in executions by such guards and assistants as he deems necessary, and request and permit the presence of the commonwealth's attorney of the court that pronounced the sentence of the clerk, and other officers of such court, and twelve respectable citizens, including a physician and surgeon. He shall, moreover, permit the presence of the convict's counsel, such ministers of the gospel as the convict desires to be present, and such of the convict's relatives as the officer may deem prudent to admit."

The Code of Virginia laid out in exact detail the procedures for hanging a criminal; however, reality was much different. The hanging turned out to be quite a spectacle, and it caught the attention of newspapers throughout the country. More than one hundred onlookers piled into a circus tent, erected by Clarke County sheriff W.W. Smallwood, to watch the execution.

As Lippkin stood on the scaffold awaiting his end, he confessed to the murder and quietly prayed. Resigned to his fate and confident in what the Bible said awaited him on the other side, the fifty-seven-year-old Lippkin calmly met his death.

Around the time of Lippkin's hanging, a wave of violence swept through Clarke County. During the week leading up to Lippkin's execution, the small county jail held a total of four men charged with murder. The court sentenced Joseph Copenhaver to twelve years in the penitentiary for killing his wife. The day before Lippkin's execution, the court convicted Benjamin

Chamblin of murdering his mistress and sentenced him to eighteen years in the penitentiary. Charged with the murder of John Krombly, Carl Carlisle awaited his trial in the county jail.

It is unclear why the county executed Lippkin for the crime of murder while Chamblin and Copenhaver, both of whom were also convicted of murder, were to serve a combined thirty years in prison. Perhaps premeditation, or the lack thereof, played a role in the sentencing, and there may have been other factors in the decisions. Nevertheless, the differences in the punishments do seem noteworthy.

The same day that Lippkin was executed for his crime, a nearly identical scene unfolded one hundred miles away, in Annapolis, Maryland. Here, another black man, Julius Cooper, who also shot a man to death, paid for his crimes with his life. It is eerie to think that two men, separated by only a short distance, committed almost identical crimes and suffered the same fate on the very same day.

Criminals are not the only people whose tragic lives ended prematurely by hanging at the courthouse grounds. A suicide occurred on the premises of what is now the sheriff's office and 911 communications center. There are whispers to this day among those who have worked in the building of the person who hanged themselves in one of the rooms.

Much of the bad energy in and around the courthouse—undoubtedly left behind from hangings and from murderers who spent time confined in the small jail—has probably spilled over into areas neighboring the courthouse grounds. Taking a late-night stroll in the vicinity can have an unsettling effect.

Across the street from the courthouse, at the Episcopal church, there is a cemetery known for hauntings. Perhaps trauma from things that went on across the street is to blame, or maybe the cemetery has its own spiritual baggage—many cemeteries do. Some people have claimed to feel an unexplained presence there and to have the feeling that someone, or something, is watching them. There have been reports of the appearance of apparitions in the cemetery. The occasional unwitting visitor has photographed a specter as they wandered the graveyard.

While conducting research for this book, I interviewed a witness who snapped a picture of a ghost in the cemetery. As is often the case, the witness did not see anything strange beforehand, but later, while reviewing the photographs she had taken on the grounds, the image of a man dressed in what looked to be nineteenth-century cavalry officer's attire was present in one of the pictures. The witness sent a copy of the image to me; it had all the

Grace Episcopal Church was established in 1832. The cemetery on its grounds is known for paranormal activity. *Courtesy of the author.*

indications of being authentic. The mysterious figure wore a wide-brimmed hat and sported a jacket that appeared to have a gold-colored decorative shoulder piece.

Most people do not like to go anywhere near a courthouse; the very thought makes many feel uneasy. With the haunted history of the Clarke County Courthouse, there is all the more reason to try to avoid a court date.

5
OTHER BERRYVILLE HAUNTS

With a legacy that stretches back to colonial times, Berryville rightfully has more than its share of haunted history. However, the large antebellum homes and timeworn clapboard houses do not have a monopoly on ghost stories. More than a few hauntings take place in the nondescript houses that line the streets of Berryville. There are also hauntings in places that few would expect: a ghost frequents a warehouse in town, a mysterious entity lurks in the woods of a nearby park and newly built homes are not immune to strange activity. These hauntings, when paired with the many historical haunts around town discussed earlier, prove that the small town of Berryville has all the bases covered concerning the paranormal.

A House on Walnut Street

The patriarch of a Clarke County family built a house on Walnut Street in the 1950s. Now, over sixty years later, members of the family spanning three generations have come forward with ghostly stories from their time in the home. The concentration of strange activity occurred in two main areas: the basement and "Nay Nay's bedroom." To give a little background that may help explain the hauntings, Nay Nay died in her bedroom some years before the odd activity started taking place.

Most anyone who has ever slept in Nay Nay's bedroom has some sort of story to tell. The sounds of murmuring voices and faint footsteps plagued the room late at night. Strange shadows would also make their way across the walls in the dead of night. The moving shadows gave off the sensation of a breeze—as if someone had passed by. Family members also heard scratching sounds in the home; the sounds came from a door in Nay Nay's bedroom that leads to the basement. Interestingly, the scratching occurred during times when no pets were present in the home.

Jodi Tiller recalled a night when she slept in Nay Nay's bedroom: "I remember hearing footsteps at the foot of the bed, and I could feel a breeze." Whatever or whomever was walking in the bedroom must have decided to stop and have a seat on the bed. "I felt a puff of air and pressure at the end of the bed, like someone sat down on it," she said.

The sound of footsteps awakened Sharon and Eric Clark late one night. It reminded them of the noise that hard-soled shoes make against a wooden floor. Once up and awake, they looked throughout the house for the source of the sound—there was nothing. Sharon recounted, "I knew we weren't dreaming because after we went back to bed and were sitting up, it happened again."

Stefanie Hess recalled an experience in Nay Nay's bedroom reminiscent of something out of the *Poltergeist* movie series. She was in the bed, and suddenly the three doors in the room went berserk. "One door would open and shut, then the next one, and then the third one did it, too," said Stefanie. "They did it in a sequence: one, two, and three," she said, "and it went on like that for about a minute." Oddly enough, Stefanie was not scared by the event. "I remember it didn't really scare me," she recalled. "In fact, nobody really got scared by anything in the house." Stefanie shrugged her shoulders and said, "It was always just one of those things."

There was one family member who did get a bit of a scare in the house: Dave. Dave grew up several hours from Berryville and moved west as an adult, so he had not spent time in the house before. In the early 2000s, he moved to the area from the West Coast and spent some time in the house as he was getting settled in. Like the other members of the family, Dave would have strange experiences of his own—only he was not prepared for them. Dave recalled one such instance. "I had just moved here and was getting settled in. So, I was home by myself; everyone else had left for work." He continued, "All of a sudden I heard the toilet flush." Perplexed by the incident, Dave started calling around. He said, "I knew I was alone, but just to doublecheck I called and made sure everyone had left. They had." To

Dave's surprise, this sort of thing was a common occurrence. "Everyone just acted like it was just one of those things," he said. "I wasn't about to go opening any doors and looking around; it scared me!"

It seems that Bethanie, the youngest of the family who lived in the home, now in her late twenties, witnessed more strange activity than anyone else. It might be that she is more sensitive to the presence of spirits, or she could have been more susceptible due to her young age. Whatever the case may be, Bethanie saw and heard many strange things, especially in the "god awful" basement, as she described it. "I had my computer down there, so obviously I was there a lot," she said. "Even with all the lights on, I could feel someone there with me, staring. It was like they were boring holes into me." And then there were the lights. "The lights would just flick on and off randomly," Bethanie recalled. "I thought at times it was Nanny forgetting I was down there, but she was always asleep in her room."

Nay Nay did not care much for Bethanie's music; music popular with preteens seemed to annoy her. Bethanie used to roller-skate and play music on the unfinished side of the basement. When she would press play on the cassette player and skate away, the music would stop. She would skate back over and restart it, and as she skated away, it would cut off again. "I always just figured Nay Nay didn't approve of my music," said Bethanie.

The family used the finished side of the basement as a gathering place during holidays and for other family events. It was here that everyone in attendance at a gathering noticed something strange and unforgettable. The man who built the home was an avid fisherman, and many years ago, he caught a massive blue marlin, which he had mounted and placed on a wall in the basement. During a family gathering in the basement, someone noticed dried blood coming from the marlin's mouth. A stream of blood had flowed out of the corner of the mouth and congealed under the fish's jaw. There was also a puddle of dried blood on the floor. When reflecting on the day, almost in unison, members of the family exclaimed, "That was crazy!"

The strangest phenomenon in the home—which could be entirely unrelated—was the prevalence of debilitating leg cramps among all the females who resided there. All the women in the home suffered unbearable cramps at night while they lived in the home; however, after moving out of the house, leg cramps rarely if ever reoccurred among the women. They all agree that *something* about the house was to blame. "I wish I knew if Nay Nay suffered from them," said Stefanie. "Maybe some way she passed them to us while we were in the house."

A Hat-Wearing Ghost and a Ghost in a Hoodie

As mentioned in the opening of this chapter, hauntings in Berryville do not limit themselves to houses and historic buildings. A warehouse in town that has been in operation for many years under several different owners has a history of hauntings. In fact, a former worker at the facility was scared to be there after hours, especially when the lights were off. Another former worker said that she saw the apparition of a man wearing a dark, hooded sweatshirt several times in the warehouse. She claimed that a fellow coworker had also seen the ghost.

As evidenced by the house on Walnut Street, historic homes are not the only haunted houses in and around Berryville. Hauntings manifest themselves even in newly constructed homes; perhaps this is a by-product of traumatic events that occurred in the area that left negative energy behind for future generations. Homes and buildings come and go, but in some cases, spirits seem to be tied to the land itself. In these instances, ghosts from prior residences become squatters in the new houses. A story comes from one such home in Berryville located in Darby Brook, a newer subdivision.

The strange activity in this home seemed to confine itself to the master bedroom; here, the homeowner has observed several strange entities, including that of a little girl and an old woman. She spotted both ghosts near the bed. Perhaps the most frightening encounter occurred when she noticed the figure of a man standing across the bedroom; this entity sported a distinctive hat.

Without jumping to conclusions from this one instance or reading too much into the description of the entity, it is easy for a student of the paranormal to see a parallel with the infamous "Hat Man"—a shadowy and malevolent entity.

Who, or what, is the Hat Man? Many in the paranormal community believe that the Hat Man is a hat-wearing variation of a "shadow person." What, then, is a shadow person? Shadow people really are what their name implies—living masses of shadows comprising a humanoid form. Like shadows, shadow people appear to be almost two-dimensional black masses. Unlike shadows, shadow people are malevolent, lifelike entities. Most think that shadow people are not the spirits of deceased humans. They may even come from another dimension.

People all over the world have seen the Hat Man—and seen him often. A traumatic life event sometimes precedes his appearance. He is also known for showing up during difficult emotional and physical times in a person's life, though this is not always the case. Unlike some spirits or entities that can be friendly and even comforting (as in a case of a visitation from a deceased loved one), experiences with the Hat Man (and shadow people) seem to be overwhelmingly negative.

The Hat Man is usually content to watch people sleep. In tale after tale, an unfortunate person awakens to see a shadowy figure in a hat—sometimes with glowing red eyes—staring at them. Witnesses have described the intruder's hat as a top hat, a fedora, a wide-brimmed hat and sometimes even a cowboy hat. Some eyewitnesses have claimed the Hat Man dresses in old-fashioned garb such as a cape or a long trench coat. The clothing is black, of course, and often described as being "too black," as if the color has an otherworldly quality to it.

Other Haunts

The lady who reported the strange activity in her Darby Brook home lived in a house on Liberty Street before moving to the subdivision. The houses on Liberty Street are old, though not hundreds of years old like some of the historic homes of Berryville. Still, many of these houses are old enough to have quite a bit of history to them. A multitude of owners may have come and gone, and many life events have taken place in these houses, perhaps enough for paranormal activity to manifest itself. This was the case in her house.

She spoke of a ghostly woman who haunted the premises and mentioned two encounters with the spirit. One day, she saw the apparition of a woman in the hallway looking into one of the bedrooms. During another experience, she heard the spirit call her name while she was in the kitchen.

There are at least two houses along Boom Road that have had strange activity take place inside the walls. Of particular interest is that one of those homes had something supernatural ooze through the walls. A former resident of the house witnessed some sort of substance she described as brown in color that would suddenly appear on a wall in her bathroom. On those occasions, when the strange substance would start seeping through the wall, no matter how hard she tried, she could not get it clean. The witness lived in the house in the mid-1980s, well before the advent of smartphones and the present age in which most everyone has instant access to a camera.

Unfortunately, she said—almost apologetically—that she was never able to photograph or film the supernatural ooze.

What was the strange substance that oozed from the walls? As strange as it may sound, the appearance of weird, goopy substances (of any color) occurs more frequently in homes that experience paranormal activity than most folks would imagine. Paranormal researchers often refer to these mystery substances as ectoplasm.

The 1984 movie *Ghostbusters* first popularized ectoplasm; mischievous ghosts in the film left slimy residue where they had been and even slimed the members of the Ghostbusters team who were on their trail. The roots of ectoplasm, however, go back to the Spiritualist movement of the late nineteenth and early twentieth centuries. During seances, a strange substance would come from the mouth, ear or other orifice of a medium whom spirits supposedly used to interact in the physical world. Faces of the spirits would appear in the substance while the medium was in a trance-like state. This phenomenon has largely been debunked; most mediums who emitted ectoplasm were actually participating in a hoax using stage props and other techniques.

Slimy fictional ghosts and hoaxer mediums aside, ectoplasm, or whatever you would like to call it, is a staple in the world of the paranormal. Some researchers believe that ectoplasm is simply another manifestation of spiritual energy, in the same way that cold spots or apparitions appear. In other words, the strange substance that oozed from the walls of the house on Boom Road was simply evidence that some sort of spirit was present in the home. And there certainly was a spirit in the home—the spirit of a large man. The witness recalled an encounter in which she observed a large-framed man in a flannel shirt sitting on the couch. She described him as being a big man wearing farmer clothes.

Before I conclude this chapter, there is a story to add that does not necessarily pertain to hauntings but is strange and frightening nevertheless. A lady was walking through the woods on the fitness trail at Chet Hobart Park when she had a bizarre encounter. It was nearing dusk, and she saw something in the trees—something huge. "It was really big like a bear, but it wasn't a bear," she said. "It was kind of like Bigfoot." The strange creature was lightly colored, according to the witness. If it isn't scary enough thinking of a Bigfoot-like creature stalking the woods of a local park, there is more: it had red eyes—large, glowing red eyes.

As noted previously, Clarke County has had a few documented Bigfoot sightings over the years; however, none mention glowing red eyes. This aspect of the sighting seems to cross over into the supernatural realm, although this trait is not entirely unknown in Bigfoot reports. In fact, northwestern New Jersey is home to a "Bigfoot variant" that locals call Big Red Eye because of its massive, glowing eyes. Big Red Eye spends the night belting out bloodcurdling screams and has a penchant for killing chickens and other livestock. Like so many people from New Jersey, New York, Pennsylvania and other northeastern states, did Big Red Eye also pack up and move to Clarke County?

In closing, the small town of Berryville is a great place to live and to raise a family. As detailed throughout the book, the charming town is rich in both hauntings and history. Perhaps it is a love for the unique town that keeps so many spirits behind, or it might be the traumatic events of the past that cause them to linger. A person writing in a local Facebook group might have summed up Berryville's haunted streets best: "You may be walking with a spirit and not know it."

6
CARTER HALL AND LONG BRANCH

The Burwell family played a major role in the early days of what would become Clarke County, and Virginia as a whole. The Burwells were a "first family," an original colonial Virginia family. They were Tidewater planters and esteemed members of the old southern aristocracy—blue bloods of the New World. It is families such as the Burwells that the term *old money* came to represent.

Virginia governor Alexander Spotswood complained about the influence of the Burwell family in Virginia politics. So many Burwells had married into Virginia political circles that Spotswood grumbled: "The greater part of present Council are related to the Family of Burwells....[T]here will be no less than seven so near related that they will go off the Bench whenever a Cause of the Burwells come to be tried."

The sixth president of the United States, John Quincy Adams, described the Burwells in a most unflattering way. In his mind, they were politically simplistic and typical of Virginia aristocrats: forthright, bland and somewhat impetuous. That notwithstanding, the legacy of the Burwells lives on to this day throughout vast portions of the state.

The Burwell influence in the Shenandoah Valley goes back to the days of Robert "King" Carter. Carter served as Lord Fairfax's agent for the lease and sale of his unoccupied lands west of the Blue Ridge. He deeded land in present-day Warren, Frederick and Clarke Counties totaling fifty thousand acres to his sons and grandsons. In present-day Clarke County, Robert Carter Burwell inherited the land where Long Branch came to be.

Robert "King" Carter served as agent for the Northern Neck Proprietary and secured tens of thousands of acres for his children and grandchildren. *Public domain image. Wikimedia Commons.*

The land where Carter Hall now stands went to Nathaniel Burwell, of James City County.

These two stately homes, Carter Hall and Long Branch, on opposite sides of U.S. Route 50 in Millwood, are the first to come to mind when thinking of Clarke County's antebellum homes. Both are magnificent, and both sit on pristine tracts of land—arguably the most beautiful land that Virginia has to offer.

Carter Hall

Now, Lucy, you can weep for your dear George,
and I can weep for my beloved Sucky.
—Nathaniel Burwell to his bride, Lucy Baylor, after their wedding ceremony

Nathaniel Burwell was born in 1750 at Carter's Grove, a large plantation near Williamsburg. Burwell served three terms in the Virginia House of Delegates. He was elected to the Virginia Ratifying Convention, where he voted in favor of the ratification of the Constitution of the United States of America.

In 1785, Burwell began raising cattle and growing wheat on his inherited land in present-day Clarke County. He split his time between his Shenandoah lands and Carter's Grove. When the construction of Carter Hall was complete, he moved to the Valley permanently in 1792. Being a savvy businessman, Burwell, along with his neighbor Daniel Morgan, established a mill nearby for which the community of Millwood takes its name.

Burwell married twice and fathered sixteen children, eight with each wife. In 1772, he married Susanna Grymes, the love of his life. Burwell's

Nathaniel Burwell and Daniel Morgan partnered to build this mill that made the community of Millwood a thriving commercial center. The Burwell-Morgan Mill is a stone's throw from Carter Hall. *Courtesy of the author.*

devotion to Susanna was deep. However, the marriage would end in 1788, when Susanna suffered a premature death at the age of thirty-seven. Crushed by the loss, Burwell simply could not bear it alone. Robert A. Lancaster's book *Historic Virginia Homes and Churches*, published in 1915, gives the following account:

> After her death, he was so bereaved that he found it impossible to bear his grief without a companion in misery and cast about to find one who had been similarly afflicted, and could, therefore, sympathize with him. Finally, he went to Rosewell and asked Governor John Page to send for his half-sister, Mrs. George Baylor, who was a young and beautiful widow, that he might marry her. She came, but promptly rejected the disconsolate widower's proposal. "Lucy," he remonstrated, "you do not know what is good for you; your brother John and I arranged it all before you came." That seemed to settle the matter, and the wedding soon took place. After the ceremony the bridegroom said, "Now, Lucy, you can weep for your dear George, and I will weep for my beloved Sucky."

Nathaniel Burwell and his bride, Lucy, would go on to live together at Carter Hall. It is unclear how long the pair spent mourning their former lovers, or if they ever stopped. Nathaniel passed away in 1814, and Lucy died in 1843. Nathaniel and Lucy, as well as a host of other Burwells and extended family, are laid to rest in the Burwell family cemetery at Old Chapel in Millwood. Other notable burials at the cemetery include Virginia governor Edmund Randolph and John Esteen Cooke, a novelist who also served as an officer in the Confederate States army.

Old Chapel holds the distinction of being the oldest Episcopal church in continuous use west of the Blue Ridge. A visit to the chapel and the cemetery bring the past to life; a more complete representation of first Virginia families would be hard to find.

When Nathaniel Burwell died, he left Carter Hall to his son George. It was George who added the impressive and iconic portico to the home. Later, George would undergo a cataract operation performed by Confederate general Stonewall Jackson's surgeon on the portico. Carter Hall would serve as Jackson's headquarters beginning in the fall of 1862. Jackson rejected Burwell's invitation to stay inside the home, opting instead to camp outside with his troops.

Carter Hall would remain in the Burwell family until 1902, when Eban Richards of St. Louis bought the estate. Carter Hall came back to the Burwell

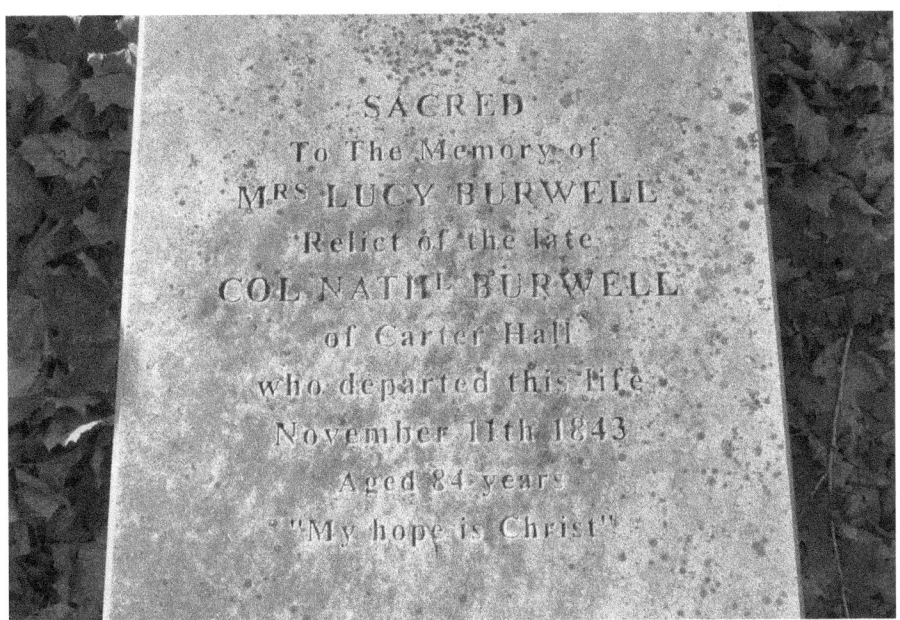

The gravestone of Lucy Burwell. *Courtesy of the author.*

The gravestone of Nathaniel Burwell. *Courtesy of the author.*

The state erected this historical marker that commemorates Old Chapel. *Courtesy of the author.*

family in 1908, when the Richards family sold it to Townsend Burwell. In 1930, Carter Hall once again left the Burwells when Gerard Lambert purchased the estate and made extensive renovations to the home. Today, Carter Hall is the headquarters of Project Hope, a nonprofit international healthcare organization.

Nathaniel Burwell was known for traveling about in an imposing coach. The coach was immense in size with a large box; a coachman and footman accompanied the vehicle. Equipped with huge wheels that were able to withstand the road conditions of the day, the massive vehicle could ride through mud and deep ruts without tipping or getting stuck. It was in a carriage such as this that Burwell traveled across the state to Rosewell to ask for Lucy Baylor's hand in marriage. It is quite the coincidence, then, that numerous reports of a mysterious, ghostly coach that matches the descriptions of Burwell's coach have been given by a long list of owners and visitors at Carter Hall throughout the decades. Even into the present day, former Project Hope employees have heard the coach.

In one of the most often-cited stories, Lucy Burwell Jolliffe and her two sons had an encounter with the phantom coach while visiting Carter Hall.

Right: A portrait of Confederate lieutenant general Thomas Jonathan "Stonewall" Jackson. *From the Library of Congress Civil War Photographs, 1861–1865.*

Below: Carter Hall, a splendid antebellum home, served as General Stonewall Jackson's headquarters during the War Between the States. Today, the nonprofit organization Project Hope owns the property. *Courtesy of the author.*

Marguerite Du Pont Lee recounted the incredible story in her book *Virginia Ghosts*, published in 1966:

> *One night sitting before the fire in the dining room, they heard the sound of a carriage being driven to the front door. Taking a candle, Mrs. Jolliffe followed by her sons, opened the door and all three saw a big old-fashioned coach with heavy wheels, two large horses, and a coachman and footman high upon the box. They could see someone was in the carriage. The*

footman jumped down, opened the door, letting down the steps. No one descended! Before their astonished gaze, he put up the steps, closed the door, and jumping to his seat beside the coachman, the crack of the whip was plainly heard as the great lumbering vehicle disappeared into the night.

Former Carter Hall owner and resident Townsend Burwell, who lived in the home in the early twentieth century, said, "Several times I have heard the arrival of a vehicle at the front door and later discovered that nothing was really there!" Burwell was skeptical of the idea that phantom horses were pulling a spectral coach occupied by spirits. He sought out a natural explanation and may have found one in a limestone cave that runs along the property. Burwell is credited with the following statement:

Unlike most ghosts, this one has a scientific reason for being. Often enough, even to this day, a coach may be heard to rumble up to the portico of the house and the old-fashioned folding steps may be heard bumping down as they are unfolded. It is, of course, very probable that the cave extends under the house and on to the west until it passes beneath the highway. Certain it is, that the road sounds queerly hollow at a certain point, and the unbelieving maintain that the sound of the coach is only that of a truck or wagon passing over the hollow place in the highroad, and that the sound is carried by the cave to the earth under the house a quarter of a mile away.

Townsend Burwell's explanation could go a long way toward explaining the eerie sound of the coach's arrival to the front of Carter Hall. It falls short, however, in explaining actual sightings of the mysterious coach and its occupants. It also fails to address other types of strange activity taking place on the grounds.

Carter Hall began with an aura of sadness; Nathaniel and Lucy's marriage was born out of grief. All accounts seem to indicate that Nathaniel Burwell never got over the loss of his first wife. Years of heavy grief, such strong emotion, is something that could certainly remain in a home long after its occupants depart this world. It is not at all uncommon for a home—or any structure, for that matter—two hundred or more years old to have a fair amount of strange activity taking place within its walls. Owners come and go; children are born and raised, and they leave; life stories of families unfold many times over; death occurs, sometimes tragically. The life experiences of so many people seem to leave behind energy. Whatever this energy is, it seems to become one with the walls of the structure; the very soil underneath

This historical marker sits at the entrance to Carter Hall. *Courtesy of the author.*

the home absorbs this energy. Carter Hall is no exception. This allows for unexplainable activity to occur far into the future.

A former housekeeper at Carter Hall has recounted several instances of strange activity that she witnessed while performing her duties. In one of the encounters, she became locked in one of the large spaces used as a pantry on a lower level of the home. While she was in the pantry, the door closed behind her, and it took several attempts to get it open and exit the space. The unusual part? There were no locks on the door; it was as if something was holding the door in place.

The former housekeeper has also shared stories of a dumbwaiter that has a mind of its own. The kitchen of the home is located on a lower level, and the dumbwaiter runs from there to a formal dining room upstairs. On many occasions, the dumbwaiter has randomly moved up and down by itself.

A painting in a formal sitting room in Carter Hall has watched many people walk by over the years. The large painting depicts a person on horseback, and according to former Project Hope employees, the eyes of the person move and even follow those who walk by. Having once seen the painting, I am reminded of another such painting I have seen, also with wandering eyes: a portrait of the philanthropist Mary Moody Northen that hangs in the lobby of the Mountain Lake Lodge in Giles County, Virginia. A skeptic would probably argue that the moving eyes on the paintings are nothing more than optical illusions. But, given that witnesses have observed paranormal activity in both locations over the decades, an otherworldly answer may be a better fit.

Long Branch

In 1788, Robert Carter Burwell inherited one thousand acres from his grandfather along a stream known as Long Branch. Here, he established what would go on to be one of today's most recognizable plantations and homes in all of Clarke County. The industrious Burwell started growing wheat on the land, and in 1811, work on an elaborate home also began. The design was largely based on the recommendations of Benjamin Henry Latrobe, who twice served in the prestigious appointment of the Architect of the Capitol.

The majestic Long Branch sits on some of the most beautiful land Virginia has to offer. *Courtesy of the author.*

In the summer of 1813, Burwell left his home at Long Branch to serve his country in the War of 1812. This would be the last he saw of his beloved home. While stationed in Norfolk, Virginia, Burwell contracted typhoid, from which he died.

Burwell left Long Branch to his sister, Sarah Nelson, and her husband, Philip. The Nelsons sold the property in 1842 to their nephew Hugh Mortimer Nelson. Before the Civil War, Nelson was a delegate to the Virginia secession convention; he was strongly opposed to Virginia leaving the Union. He said the following in a speech:

> *I come from the banks of the sparkling Shenandoah, "Daughter of the stars," as its name imports. I live within a day's march of the Thermopylae of Virginia. That valley, now beautiful and peaceful "as the Vale of Tempe, may be a very Bochim—a place of weeping." Those green fields, where now "lowing herds wind slowly o'er the lea," may become fields of blood. Can you blame me, then, if I wish to try all peaceful means, consistent with Virginia honor, of obtaining our rights, before I try the last resort?*

Although he opposed secession, when war broke out between the states, Nelson sided with Virginia and commanded the Sixth Virginia Cavalry. Nelson would become one of more than 620,000 soldiers who lost their lives in the conflict after succumbing to an infection from a wound he suffered in combat.

Long Branch stayed in the hands of the Nelson family until the 1950s, when Abram and Dorothy Hewitt bought the property for an unthinkable price today: $125,000.

In 1968, Long Branch became a Virginia Historic Landmark. A year later, the National Register of Historic Places listed Long Branch in its vast registry. Today, Long Branch welcomes visitors, and guided tours are available thanks to the efforts of Harry Z. Isaacs. Isaacs purchased the property in 1986 and gave the home the refurbishment that it so desperately needed. Before his death, he created and endowed the Harry Z. Isaacs Foundation, whose mission is "to hold, preserve, maintain and operate Long Branch Farm…for charitable purposes."

With a history than spans two centuries, Long Branch is the type of home where the paranormal enthusiast would expect anomalous activity to take place. This is exactly the case. One of the most commonly cited strange happenings is a servant's bell that seemingly has a mind of its

This finely crafted horse hitch is still in place at Long Branch. *Courtesy of the author.*

own. The former room of Adelaide Nelson is equipped with servant's bell that rings on its own at random times. A skeptic might argue that an electrical issue is to blame; however, other odd occurrences take place in the house as well.

One such oddity is the sound of footsteps when no one is present. A phantom walks the upper level of the home, and its footsteps echo throughout the house. The ghostly footsteps make a distinctive sound, like the way shoes with wooden soles sound when they click against a wood floor.

Like so many other homes where paranormal activity takes place, the basement of Long Branch has also been a source for the strange. Basements are often associated with cold spots, voices, orbs, moving objects and any number of other strange phenomena. Likewise, at Long Branch, people occasionally hear the voice of a man when no one is present to utter the sounds.

Closing Thoughts

The Burwells' roots run deep in Virginia, and their legacy still remains in the stately homes and pristine tracts of land scattered about the state. Readers of this book, however, probably appreciate most the paranormal activity attached to the old Burwell homesteads. It is interesting to note that even Carter Grove, the home and planation built for Carter Burwell—Nathaniel Burwell's father—is also known for hauntings. According to rumor, the apparition of Jim, who was a slave on the plantation, can be seen wandering the premises at night. Legend holds that Burwell frequently rented Jim out to the governor of Williamsburg. One night, Jim walked back to Carter Grove to visit with his family. Unfortunately, he returned to find that his family had been rented out, too, and he never saw them again. To this day, Jim still makes the long and agonizing walk, searching in vain for his loved ones.

Today, Carter Hall and Long Branch, and Carter's Grove near Williamsburg, stand as testaments to Old Virginia. There are two sides to that coin. Heads is southern hospitality, picturesque landscapes, stunning architecture and the prestige of Virginia's first families. Tails is much darker: the stark reminders of the plantation lifestyle is ever-present. Then there are the ghosts—there are always the ghosts.

7
HAUNTS ALONG THE RIVER

Never since the sound of the rifle was heard in this beautiful Valley have the "sea green" waters of the Shenandoah have been so reddened.
—North Carolina Standard, *August 10, 1864*

There is something about water, particularly rivers, that seems to attract unexplained phenomena. For reasons that we are incapable of understanding, a disproportionate number of ghosts and UFOs are spotted alongside them. Do these entities access water as a travel route? Cryptid sightings also occur along water sources in greater numbers than most would expect. From Bigfoot to chupacabras, black panthers to Sheepsquatch, winged humanoids to dogmen and many more, waterways attract these mysterious beasts much more so than known animals. Some suggest that water acts as a conduit for spiritual and supernatural energy. Certainly, no one will prove (or disprove) this theory anytime soon, given our current understanding of the world around us. But, if there is any merit to this idea, how would it bode for a river that cuts through a vast section of land renowned for wartime activity? What would this mean for a river whose waters ran red as former countrymen tore into one another's flesh with musket balls, bayonets, sabers and cannon fire? And what would it mean for a river that saw an entire tribe wiped out long before the United States became a nation?

Almost two centuries before the states went to war with one another, warring native tribes spilled blood on the banks of the Shenandoah River.

Aldine Magazine printed an engraving by J.D. Woodward titled *Moonlight on the Shenandoah* in a July 1873 issue. *Public domain image. Wikimedia Commons.*

The Catawba annihilated the Senedo tribe sometime between 1650 and 1700, according to historians. We know very little about the Senedo tribe. What we do know is that the Senedo are an extinct people; they lived along portions of the Shenandoah and most likely spoke an Iroquoian language. There are accounts from the Shenandoah Valley in early colonial times in which a few Senedo men claimed to have survived a massacre by the Catawba.

Violence is not the only cause of death on the Shenandoah. Like most any river, unexpected and unseen hazards are always lurking; even the calmest of waters are fraught with danger. Currents can be deceivingly strong; shallow waters can suddenly give way to abyss-like depths; slippery rocks and treacherous footing have felled many. Recreation can turn deadly—more than a few boating and tubing accidents have taken place on the Shenandoah.

There is no way to know how many people have had their lives cut short in the waters of the Shenandoah. What can be known, however, is that there are more than a few restless spirits crossing the river and wandering its banks. Clarke County residents and others who have spent time along the river have spotted many of these apparitions.

Phantom Soldiers of the Shenandoah River

There have long been reports in Clarke County of ghostly soldiers along the Shenandoah River. Unwitting observers have spotted spectral fighters crossing the river. Then there are the noises—many have heard shouts and cries from the wounded along the river. Some have said that they have heard the wounded crying out while driving late at night past Springsbury Farm, just a stone's throw from the river. Considering the fierce fighting that took place in northern Virginia during the Civil War and that the Shenandoah served as a natural barrier against Union forces shortly after crossing the Blue Ridge, it is not surprising that the spirits of the fallen still linger along the banks of the Shenandoah more than a century and a half later.

Tragedy befell the Seventy-Fifth Regiment, Pennsylvania Volunteer Infantry, a unit almost entirely composed of German immigrants and German-speaking residents of Philadelphia, in April 1862. The regiment was ordered to cross the Shenandoah at Berry's Ferry, the modern-day location of the U.S. 50 bridge, in pursuit of General Stonewall Jackson's troops. Crossing was treacherous, as several days of snow and rain had caused the waters to swell. Samuel P. Bates, in his work *History of Pennsylvania Volunteers, 1861–5, Vol. 2*, recounts the following:

> *Several rafts were constructed to cross the troops. The river was high, and the current rapid. Company D, the skirmish company, crossed in safety, when, to save time, an old ferry boat which had been partly burned by the enemy, was repaired, and a rope stretched across the stream to guide it. Companies I and K embarked, and when near the middle of the stream, the boat swamped and suddenly began to sink. It was a moment of terror. A shriek of agony rent the air as they were suddenly engulfed. Scores of knapsacks covering the surface of the water were all that was visible of the unfortunate men as they floated, thus burdened, in the river. Captain Christian Wyck, of company K, Lieutenant Adolf Winter, of company I, First Sergeant Joseph Tiedemann, of company K, and fifty enlisted men were drowned. Sergeant Tiedemann, an expert swimmer, sacrificed his life in a vain attempt to save that of his Captain.*

In all, fifty-three men lost their lives. The force that remained on the eastern bank marched toward the present-day Route 7 bridge and crossed the river at Snicker's Ferry. Two years later, much bloodshed occurred in this area during the Battle of Cool Spring.

Confederate lieutenant general Jubal Anderson Early commanded the Army of the Valley during the Valley campaigns of 1864. *From the Library of Congress Civil War Photographs, 1861–1865.*

The Battle of Cool Spring was set into motion after Lieutenant General Jubal Early failed to take control of Washington, D.C., at the Battle of Fort Stevens. After the unsuccessful incursion into enemy territory, he retired to the Shenandoah Valley and set up his headquarters in Berryville. President Lincoln ordered an immediate pursuit of the Confederates, and Major General Horatio Wright led the pursuing force. Brigadier General George Crook and a contingent of his command joined General Wright.

While en route to Berryville, General Early left a large force behind to guard the Shenandoah's major river crossings. On July 17, 1864, while trying to cross the river, the Confederates repulsed the Union forces at Castleman's Ferry.

The following day, a Confederate deserter led a small Union force under the command of Colonel Joseph Thoburn to "the Retreat," the home of Judge Richard Parker. It was Judge Parker who presided over the trial of the staunch abolitionist John Brown after his raid on the Federal arsenal at Harpers Ferry. Brown was hanged in Charles Town in December 1859; rumor holds that Parker signed Brown's death warrant on the lawn of the Retreat.

At Judge Parker's property, the Union troops were able to access a shallow stretch of river and crossed the Shenandoah with ease, moving across virtually undetected. After crossing, the Federal troops established a line behind a stone fence on Cool Spring Farm.

When Confederate major generals John C. Breckinridge and John B. Gordon learned of the Union crossing from their pickets, Gordon moved a division toward the Union position. Breckinridge ordered Brigadier General Gabriel C. Wharton and Major General Robert E. Rhodes to also join in the offensive.

The superior numbers of Confederate troops forced a Union retreat. In the confusion, many Union soldiers missed the crossing and found themselves thrust into "Parker's Hole"—a seemingly bottomless section of river—where they drowned. For fifty years or more after the battle,

The Retreat is the former home of Judge Richard Parker. Union forces crossed the Shenandoah River on Parker's property at the Battle of Cool Spring. *Courtesy of the author.*

It is hard to imagine that this tranquil setting, at Holy Cross Abbey, was the site of intense conflict and bloodshed during the Battle of Cool Spring. *Courtesy of the author.*

Holy Cross Abbey, a quaint community of Cistercian monks, was the scene of a major battle during the summer of 1864. *Courtesy of the author.*

fishermen would drag muskets up off of the river bottom—a grim reminder of those who had fallen.

When the fighting ended, there were 422 casualties on the Union side. The Confederate forces suffered 397 casualties.

Today, the battle site is preserved on both sides of the river; the old Cool Spring Farm is part of Holy Cross Abbey, a monastery of the Catholic Order of Cistercians of the Strict Observance. Across the river, where the Union forces made their crossing, lies Shenandoah University's Shenandoah River Campus at Cool Spring Battlefield. Though this land has been preserved for future generations, fighting continues among the spirits, which are unaware that the war has ended.

THE CHILLY HOLLOW MONSTER

Driving east on Route 7 shortly before reaching the Shenandoah and taking a right at Nalls Farm Market will put you on Chilly Hollow Road. Back in the day, moonshiners plied their trade in the woods along this narrow

Nalls Farm Market sits at the intersection of Route 7 and Chilly Hollow Road. *Courtesy of the author.*

country road. These days, the woods nestled between Chilly Hollow Road and Quarry Road is home to a local monster legend.

Locals tell that late at night—and only at night—horrible screams occasionally emanate from the woods. The sounds are bloodcurdling and resemble a woman loudly shrieking in terror. It is unclear if anyone has ever seen the monster, or if it is even a monster at all. It could just be a bobcat crying out. It might be that an old-timer made up a tale and attributed a bobcat's scream to a monster, thus giving birth to the "Chilly Hollow Monster." It is worth pointing out, however, that high-pitched screams coming from the woods—particularly those that sound like a woman shrieking—have been associated with ghost lore for centuries. The banshees of Irish mythology were disembodied female spirits who loudly wailed and shrieked. This is where the old saying "screaming like a banshee" comes from.

Like renowned ghosts such as the banshee, various monsters all over the world are also linked to the sound of a shrieking woman in the dead of night. Today, across North America, many witnesses claiming to have had an encounter with Bigfoot have heard frightening screams in the forest. A witness from Florida, whose account is identical to hundreds—possibly thousands—of others, said, "It let out a terrible scream, like a woman

Could a monster be lurking in the woods along Chilly Hollow Road? *Courtesy of the author.*

screaming in horror at the top of her lungs." Continuing with the account, she said: "It sounded almost like a woman was being attacked. On the other hand, though, there's no way a person could scream that loud."

Whatever the Chilly Hollow Monster is—a bobcat, a fisher cat that wandered east, a fox, some other animal that screams or even a monster such as the legendary Bigfoot—one thing is certain: when the creature lets out its scream, the hair will stand up on anyone who hears it!

STUBBLEFIELD

Melodie Butt used to live in an old historic home near the river known as Stubblefield. Stubblefield has quite a history, as it was originally part of Springsbury Farm. Former French consul-general John Holker settled at Springsbury after the Revolutionary War. Holker brought over a priest from France and built a cottage for him on the grounds of Springsbury. The cottage underwent additions and renovations and was moved to its present location in the 1950s and became Stubblefield.

Melodie and her family came to believe that two spirits haunted Stubblefield: a woman named Catherine and a French priest from the 1800s. Judging from the sound of the stories from the home, however, there may have been other yet-to-be-identified spirits residing there as well.

Melodie recalls hearing strange voices in the home when she would do laundry in the basement. "I would hear people talking upstairs," she said, "but I could never make out what they were saying." This was perplexing to her. She recounted, "I would walk upstairs and there was no one, but I had just heard people talking!" As further confirmation that something had been there, she claims that the hair on her arms and neck would stand on end when she came upstairs after hearing the talking.

The spirit known as Catherine tended to throw things and slam doors. Melodie recalls one particular episode: "I watched a piece of wood that I had pushed into the crevice of the sunroom door fly across the floor." She went on, "Both the doors that go into the sunroom slammed shut."

A lady named Dawn visited the house, and she must have upset Catherine. Dawn, a psychic, told Melodie and a group of several others present, "She knows we are here." This scared Melodie so much that she nearly fainted.

Springsbury Farm was gifted to Casey Tree Farm, a nonprofit group based in Washington, D.C., in 2008. *Courtesy of the author.*

The ghostly Frenchman that inhabited the home put quite a scare into Melodie's children. Her six-year-old son saw a man walk into his upstairs bedroom—the spectral stranger stopped and looked at the boy before turning and walking into the bathroom. The mysterious intruder then vanished. After this happened, none of the children would sleep upstairs again.

Speaking of the upstairs, Melodie's daughter went up there one day to put something in the attic. When she moved the square piece of wood to access the attic space, something moved it back—with authority! An unseen force slammed the piece of wood back into place. Understandably, her daughter ran back downstairs.

According to Melodie, it was common for doors in the house to slam shut on their own, and as she said, "there were just so many things that happened in that home." Perhaps the greatest testament to the weirdness in the house was the effect it had on the family dog. Little Tooty would often go into the original part of the house and stare and bark—at nothing. That is, nothing visible to the human eye.

Pets, specifically dogs, seem to have a sixth sense and are able to get a peek into the "other side." There are countless stories of dogs that have a sensitivity to the supernatural and seem to detect ghosts and otherworldly entities. Obviously, dogs have stronger senses than humans, and as far as a sixth sense, that seems to be more refined, too.

Pet psychologist Marti Miller says that dogs "don't judge what is going on in the environment." In other words, dogs do not try to rationalize or deny paranormal activity in the way that humans do. Miller went on to say, "If you observe a dog standing in the corner, barking at nothing visible, then there's a good chance that he's barking at an entity, spirit, or energy that doesn't belong there."

Maybe we could all learn a thing or two from Little Tooty.

8
SLAVERY AND GHOST LORE

The institution of slavery as practiced in the antebellum South is a delicate issue to discuss and not one to take lightly. With that said, a study of the hauntings of Clarke County, or anywhere in the South, would be incomplete without a brief discussion of the role that slavery plays in ghost lore. As mentioned in the introductory chapter, much of the land in Clarke County went to the descendants of the large plantation owners from Virginia's Tidewater region. The new generation set up its own sprawling plantations and built elaborate homes throughout the county. The planter class is forever intertwined with the institution of slavery, and the practice thrived throughout the county until the Civil War.

A disproportionate number of Clarke County residents were slaves compared to the other counties that lie within the Shenandoah Valley. Moreover, per capita, Clarke County had the greatest density of slaves in Virginia west of the Blue Ridge. According to the 1860 census, there were 3,707 whites and 3,375 slaves in the county, along with 64 free people of color. By contrast, Shenandoah County, today a short drive from Clarke, had a white population of 12,827, 316 free people of color and 753 slaves. Buchanan County, tucked away in the southwestern corner of the state, where Virginia, Kentucky and West Virginia meet, had 1 free person of color, 30 slaves and a white population of 2,762.

Though small in size, Clarke County found itself at the center of a couple of noteworthy events prior to the Civil War. The first was a test of the

Fugitive Slave Act of 1850, or the "Bloodhound Law," as abolitionists called it. A decade later, a court found two slaves guilty of conspiring to start a revolt among the county's enslaved workforce.

Well before either of these events, the *Herald of Freedom* of Hagerstown, Maryland, reported that frustrated Clarke County slave owners held a meeting on January 31, 1846. The purpose of the gathering was to discuss issues facing the slaveholding community, including ways to stop their slaves from running away, ideas for making slave patrols more effective and ways to handle those who would aid and abet a fugitive slave.

Runaway Slaves

In August 1850, eight slaves fled Clarke County and made their way into Pennsylvania. Seven of William Taylor's slaves escaped on horseback; a slave named Billy, who belonged to John E. Page, joined the group. Taylor and about a dozen men were hot on the trail of the runaway slaves and pursued at least three of them all the way to Harrisburg. There, Taylor ordered Constable Solomon Snyder to arrest Billy and two of his slaves, George Brock and Samuel Wilson, for horse theft. At their trial, Judge Pearson ruled that stealing horses was not theft when used to escape enslavement. Moreover, the men on trial released the horses about thirty miles after their escape, allowing for Taylor recover them. The judge found the men not guilty and ordered their release.

Taylor and his gang tried to apprehend the runaways upon their release from jail, setting off a riot in the streets of Harrisburg. Taylor's men managed to put two of the men in handcuffs; the third escaped. Warrants were issued for the arrest of all involved in the riot. The authorities jailed all involved, including Taylor, his men, the two slaves and their defenders.

The court dropped the charges against Taylor, and he took possession of his slaves under the provisions of the newly enacted Fugitive Slave Act. The *Charleston Free Press* described the return of the slaves to Clarke County as a "gratifying spectacle": "It was somewhat a novel, though gratifying spectacle, to see two fugitive slaves homeward bound, under the charge of officers from a Free State."

The *Meadville Gazette and Journal*, a Pennsylvania newspaper, had a much different perspective on the affair:

This broadside printed by the *Virginia Free Press* advertises a reward for the capture of a slave who escaped a Clarke County plantation. *Public domain image. Wikimedia Commons.*

It must indeed be "gratifying" to the masters of slaves, not only to have their "chattels" returned to them, but the expense paid out of Uncle Sam's pocket! The commissioner gets his $10 in each case, and the officers their per diem allowance and mileage for conducting these human beings back into bondage in this land of liberty! All paid, too, by the Freeman of the North, under this odious law, to sustain Southern Slavery.

JERRY AND JOE

In January 1860, only a month after the authorities hanged John Brown in Charles Town for his attempt to bring about a slave uprising with his raid on the Federal arsenal at Harpers Ferry, Clarke County made headlines when the court convicted two slaves, named Jerry and Joe, of conspiracy. The court ruled that Joe's owner would sell him out of state; a trip to the gallows awaited Jerry on February 17, 1860.

Trouble for the pair began when a man referred to as Mr. Chamblin approached them and began making small talk. He asked who the men belonged to, how many slaves their master owned and other questions. Jerry answered the questions "with so much alacrity, that Chamblin's suspicions were aroused."

It seems that Jerry had mistaken Chamblin for one of John Brown's men. When the discussion turned to Brown's raid on Harpers Ferry, Jerry sealed his own fate. Chamblin asked what Jerry thought about the event, and he said that he was glad to hear of it. Chamblin then asked, "Why were you not there?"

Jerry responded, "Because I did not know exactly when to go."

Chamblin kept prodding, "Would you have gone if you had known?"

"Yes. And I have four sons that would have followed me," Jerry assured him. "I would be ready to go at any time."

Chamblin then asked Joe if he would go, too, and Joe said that he would. Chamblin went on to tell the pair that he was one of Brown's men; he gathered more information. Jerry and Joe shared the locations of other slaves to talk to, as well as information about the local slave patrols.

Chamblin returned in ten days and continued his conversation with Jerry. This time, Jerry allegedly divulged a plot to burn local farmhouses. The *Baltimore Sun* reported on their exchange:

> *The patrol had not been out that week, and that he and others had made a plot the night before to burn the house of Daniel H. Sowers in the dark of the moon. At that juncture Mr. Alfred Castleman appeared in sight, passing along the road, and Jerry commenced abusing him most violently to the witness, stating that he intended to burn him out himself, that he had been to Berryville the Sunday before to get matches, but could not get any. (It was proved by another witness that Jerry was in Berryville the previous Sunday.) They were then joined by the other negro, Joe, and the conversation turned upon John Brown, then in jail under sentence of death, and the possibility of rescuing him. Joe remarking that he had heard that an army was coming on to take him out of jail, "and if we join them we can take him out," to which the prisoner (Jerry) assented, provided they could stop the patrol so they could get him out.*

Chamblin turned Jerry and Joe over to the authorities, and five magistrates presided over their trial. In a unanimous decision, the court convicted the pair of conspiracy. Local newspapers lauded Chamblin's method of extracting information from Jerry and Joe as "ingenious." The *Baltimore Sun* heaped praise upon Chamblin: "Mr. Chamblin, the witness in this case, deserves the thanks of the community for having, at his own peril, ferreted out this conspiracy. Like many others who have been most true to Virginia in her hour of trial, he is a non-slaveholder."

Fortunately, the judges strongly recommended leniency for Jerry, and on February 10, 1860, one week before his scheduled execution, Governor John Letcher commuted the sentence.

Ghost Lore

Slavery and hauntings go hand in hand. And why wouldn't they? The abuse and torment inflicted on human beings take a devastating toll capable of leaving energy behind for generations; the utter despair and hopelessness of those unable to exercise their inherent right to self-determination leave a scar on the land. This can manifest itself through hauntings. From Florida to Delaware and from Texas to Maryland, over a century and a half after the Emancipation Proclamation, it is easy to find ghostly tales from the fifteen slave states. Countless former slave dormitories, basements that housed slaves, outbuildings and other structures show the classic signs of paranormal activity—phantom footsteps and voices, cold spots, objects that move on their own, flickering lights and more. Even newly constructed homes have been known to show these signs when built on land that once harbored a workforce made up of enslaved men and women.

Beth recalls a nondescript single-family home in Berryville that she lived in that was several decades old. Inexplicably, she would hear chains rattling in the attic at night. This was peculiar for many reasons, not the least of which was that the home had been in the family since its construction; there was absolutely no reason to believe that anyone had ever been chained in the attic! She recounted one instance of chain rattling that occurred late at night: "I heard boards creaking and then it sounded like one of the boards broke." She continued, "It sounded like when the board broke, it slammed down on the floor with chains rattling, like the chains were attached to the board when it fell."

Unequivocally, no one had ever found themselves shackled in the attic of the home; something must have occurred on the land before the construction of the house. Coincidentally, the house sits on a parcel of land with a long history of agricultural use—a vast orchard once stood in place of today's single-family homes. In antebellum times, slaves worked the land where the house currently sits. Without a doubt, the chains that Beth heard rattling were coming from a much darker place in time; somehow, this energy carried over into the present day.

This building, at the State Arboretum of Virginia off of Route 50, once served as a slave quarters. It is not well known for hauntings, but it is a recognizable landmark typical of slave dormitories of the day. *Courtesy of the author.*

Mark was working in an old home in the county, prepping the walls of an upstairs bedroom for painting. On the other side of the room, he opened a door and saw a narrow and steep stairwell and rickety staircase. His boss looked over and told him, "Those are the slave stairs."

"Slave stairs?" asked Mark.

"Yeah. The slaves that worked in the house stayed in the basement," the foreman replied. "They used these stairs to get to the kitchen and up here, so the owners didn't have to see them." He continued, "Lots of these old houses built before the war have these."

Mark had never been inside of a home with such a feature, at least as far as he knew, and this aroused his curiosity. His boss was hard of hearing, so when he went to work in the adjacent room, Mark started down the stairs in hopes of getting a look at the basement.

"I took a look down the stairs and it was kind of cool," said Mark, "I was just being nosey, I guess, and I decided I wanted to take a quick peek in the basement. Normally, I wouldn't have cared, but since he told me slaves used to live down there, I got kind of curious. I thought I'd run down, peek my head in, and run back up really quick before the boss noticed."

Mark started down the cramped, dark stairway. Before he could get to the basement, fear overtook him. He said, "I got the feeling someone or something was watching me. Whoever or whatever it was, didn't want me there, and I sure didn't want to push my luck."

Mark quickly retreated and headed back up the stairs and started what he should have been doing all along: working.

When Mark recalls his trip to the basement, he remembers a "heaviness" in the air; he also said a terrible feeling came over him that robbed him of his curiosity. "I never even thought about going back down. I had no interest in seeing the basement anymore!"

Tales such as these are common throughout the county, and the entire South, for that matter.

Unsurprisingly, the South is home to countless stories of slaves who have returned from the grave to torment their former masters. Conversely, there are also tales of ruthless slave owners who came back to haunt their former slaves. The Federal Writers' Project's *Slave Narratives: A Folk History of Slavery in the United States* recounted many of these tales.

Sophia Word, a former slave from Kentucky, told of Hugh White, a slave owner on a neighboring plantation. White was so cruel that two of his female slaves committed suicide. One of the women came back from the grave to torment him and stood by his bedside each night. So bothered was White that he left the home and moved to Richmond. The demons from White's past followed him despite the change of scenery, and he hanged himself sometime later.

Jane Arrington, a former slave from North Carolina, told the story of John May. Two white men beat May to death. The grave would not hold May down, however, and he took revenge on his former tormenters. Says Arrington in *Slave Narratives*: "John May come back an' wurried both of 'em. Dey could hardly sleep arter dat. Dey said dey could hear him hollerin' an' groanin' most all de time. Dese white men would groan in dere sleep an' tell John to go away. Dey would say, 'Go way John, please go away'. De other slaves wus afraid of 'em cause de ghost of John wurried 'em so bad."

Sometimes a ghost haunts a general area rather than targeting specific individuals. In the South, these are often locations where a slave was murdered or a spot where beatings regularly occurred. In some instances, a cruel owner may have denied a proper burial for a deceased slave, thereby cursing the land. Texas-born former slave Tempie Cummings recounted such a haunted area in *Slave Narratives*: "My old man say, in slavery time, when he's 21, he had to pass a place where patrols whipped slaves and had kilt some. He was sittin' on a load of fodder and there come a big light wavin' down the road and scarin' the team and the hosses drag him and near kilt him."

Also in *Slave Narratives*, Sarah Douglas told of an owner who reached out from the grave to assert her dominance over her former subjects: "Old miss was very strict on us and after she died we was so glad we had a big dance in miss's kitchen and old miss came back and slapped one of the slaves and left the print of her hand on her face. That white hand never did go away and that place was forever haunted after that."

In another tale of a slave owner who returned from the grave, recounted in *Slave Narratives*, the owner was both helpful and vengeful. He appeared before a well-liked slave and told her the location of a buried cache of treasure. Seeing the apparition frightened her, and she screamed out; with this, the ghost disappeared. When questioned about the incident by several other slaves and their pastor, she revealed the location of the treasure. The group then set off to recover the loot. As they began digging, bystanders heard the sharp crack of a whip, and the pastor cried out and dropped his shovel. The ghostly beating caused his back to become covered in welts and blood—wounds that he later died from.

An incident of physical contact with an entity occurred in Clarke County over twenty-five years ago. Thankfully, the strange experience lacked the brutality unleashed on the treasure-seeking pastor. James, who lived in Clarke County in the early 1990s, had an unsettling encounter on a cold winter night.

"I used to live on a few acres off Route 50," he said. "Sometimes I'd go over and help out my buddy on his uncle's farm nearby."

James went over late on a Saturday afternoon to help clean out an old building. After working a couple of hours, he was wrapping things up as dusk approached. "We were pretty much done and figured we'd drink a few beers," James said. "We flipped a coin to see who would stay and finish and who would run out and grab some Coors Light."

James lost the coin toss and agreed to finish up while his buddy made the beer run. "It had gotten dark, but there was enough moonlight that I could see to carry some boards over to a scrap pile they had kind of back out of the way," he said. "It was always a little creepy there in the dark, especially if you were by yourself."

The creepiness had only begun. As James carried a pallet over to the pile, something pushed him. "I swear I didn't trip, something pushed me," he said. "I damn near fell down."

James tossed the pallet on the pile and noticed a painful burning sensation on his left shoulder. "I stuck my hand under my sweatshirt, and I could feel welts," he said.

After his friend returned with the beer, the pair went into the house to watch television and have a couple of drinks. "Once we went inside, I went to the bathroom and pulled my shirt off and looked in the mirror at my shoulder," James said. "There were three long, red scratch marks."

Though unsettled, James kept the encounter to himself. "I didn't say anything about it," he recalled. "Those boys I ran with back then never would've let me hear the end of it. I'll tell you this, though: I only went back over there a couple more times and I was gone way before dark!"

What happened that night? James cannot be sure. "Most of those farms around there used to be part of really big farms that had lots of slaves," he said. "I always figured the ghost of a slave got after me. Either that, or maybe somebody that used to treat the slaves bad took a swipe at me." Struggling for answers, James said, "Maybe it was nothing." Reconsidering, he laughed and said, "Nah, it was something, but for all I know it was a big ghost cat. All I know is it scared the hell out of me."

Superstitions

Nineteenth- and early twentieth-century writings often portrayed slaves, former slaves and African Americans in general as highly superstitious and easily scared by ghost stories. This is an unfortunate characterization, considering that most any white southerners can point to an older family member—often a grandmother—who gets upset at the sight of a black cat and is vigilant in never making plans on Sunday, limiting activity as much as possible on Friday the Thirteenth, always closing an umbrella before setting foot inside and never, ever tossing a hat onto a bed. Moreover, there has always been a host of superstitions unique to the South. In fact, in 1903, the *Clarke Courier* ran a piece that appeared in newspapers across the nation titled "Southern Superstitions" that chronicled some of the commonly held beliefs in Dixie, a few of which involve ghosts:

Southern Superstitions

If you kill frogs, your cows will "go dry."
Tickling a baby will cause the child to stutter.
To throw hair combings out of the window is bad luck.
To thank a person for combing your hair will bring bad luck.
No person who touches a dead body will be haunted by its spirit.
Cut a dog's "dew claws" and it will not die from poisonous snake bite.
To kill a ghost it must be shot with a bullet made of a silver quarter dollar.
To dream of a live snake means enemies at large; of a dead snake enemies dead or powerless.
To dream of unbroken eggs signals trouble to come; if the eggs are broken, the trouble is past.
If you boast of your good health, pound wood immediately with your fist or you will become sick.
To cut a baby's finger nails will deform it. If the child is a month old, it will cause it to have fits.
To allow a child to look into a mirror before it is a month old will cause it to have trouble in teething.
A child will have a nature and disposition similar to those of the person who first takes it out of doors.
To hear a screech owl is bad luck. To prevent hearing its cry turn the pockets inside out and set the shoe soles upward.

9

LONG MARSH RUN TO EPHRATA

THE STORY OF THE GHOSTLY BEELER WIVES

And if there be someone who doubts the truth of the matter and thinks it is an old wives' tale, he ought to go to the trouble of pursuing the matter with the many eyewitnesses. For herein I call upon the testimony of my husband's children, our neighbors, people in Winchester and many inhabitants of Ephrata where the affair was settled at last.
—Eliseba Beeler

During the mid-eighteenth century, Virginia's Shenandoah Valley was little more than a vast wilderness. However, not far to the north in the Pennsylvania colony, things were getting crowded and the price of land was soaring. Unable to obtain affordable land in Pennsylvania, German and Scotch-Irish settlers began moving south into Virginia.

The eighteenth and nineteenth centuries were times of renowned religious expression in America. There were periods of "awakening" and great revival. Entirely new churches and denominations got their starts. Perhaps the most successful of these were the Church of Jesus Christ of Latter-day Saints and the Seventh-day Adventist Church. Religious expression would also push the boundaries of acceptance; Spiritualism, mysticism and breakaway sects were on the rise. Many of those seeds were sown in Pennsylvania during the 1700s. Here, there were groups of German mystics who believed the second coming of Christ was imminent, and they sought out seclusion from the world and chose to live austere lives as they waited patiently for the arrival of their Savior. As the movements grew, the affordable and sparsely populated lands in Virginia were appealing, and against this backdrop, a strange ghost story played out in 1761 along Long Marsh Run in present-day Clarke County.

The story begins in Lancaster County, Pennsylvania, at the Ephrata Cloister—a semi-monastic religious community founded by Johann Conrad Beissel. Beissel was born in 1691 and immigrated to Pennsylvania in 1720. He split from the Brethren Church where he held a leadership role and went off to live as a hermit. He was a popular and charismatic teacher, and others followed Beissel, and the Ephrata Cloister was born in 1732.

The inhabitants of the cloister worshiped on Saturday and practiced an ascetic form of devotion. Adherents to Beissel's teachings ate only one small meal a day consisting of vegetables; they ate meat only on special occasions. Six hours of sleep per night was the norm, broken into two parts, with a midnight worship service in between. Clothing consisted of a long, white robe, and members went barefoot and wore shoes only during the coldest of weather. A key tenet of the sect was celibacy—although not required, it was believed that only those who abstained from sex could achieve the highest levels of spiritual growth.

Women and men were segregated at the Ephrata Cloister. These buildings served as dormitories for the women. *Photograph by Devanie Joy. Wikimedia Commons.*

The sect welcomed believing families and married couples into the fold; they lived in houses just outside the main commune. These were known as "house holders," while the celibates—called Brothers and Sisters—lived in dormitories segregated into male and female dwellings. Life was not as austere for the house holders as it was for the celibates; they were not completely cut off from worldly comforts. Seeking greater spiritual growth, there were married couples in the community who practiced celibacy. This could become very problematic for the couple when it was not a mutually agreed upon decision. The *Chronicon*, a written history of the Ephrata Cloister, said the following about the Beeler family, which was torn apart by the act of adultery after the wife became celibate:

> *There were two young married persons in the Community of Ephrata who were anxious about their eternal welfare; but because, according to the usage of these times, the wife entered upon the practice of continence without consent of her husband, he fell into grate temptation, and at last sinned with a neighboring widow whom he had served in many ways. Because on this account he lost his fellowship with the Community, he took his children and the said widow with him to Virginia, and left his first wife in the Community. After he had three children by that widow, she died, and he married a person of noble birth, who had just arrived in the country, and who called herself Henrietta Wilhelmina von Höning, but who did not bring the best character with her into the country.*

When he lost his fellowship at Ephrata, Christopher Beeler, referred to only as C.B. in the *Chronicon*, moved to present-day Clarke County in 1740 and settled on 139 acres along Long Marsh Run with his three children and the widow of Hans Michael Schüle. His wife, Catherina, who stayed at the cloister and became Sister Esther, died the following year, enabling Beeler to legally remarry.

Beeler prospered in Virginia and amassed an enormous amount of land. Three years after settling on the banks of Long Marsh Run, he bought 500 acres that lay to the west of the Shenandoah River. Additionally, he owned a home in Alexandria and 387 acres near present-day Keyser, West Virginia.

Beeler's second wife, with whom he had three children, fell ill in 1757, and he returned with her to the cloister for medical treatment. She died there the following year, and in 1760, Beeler married his third wife, Henrietta Wilhelmina von Höning, who had recently emigrated from Germany. She came to be known as Eliseba Beeler.

Ghostly Manifestations

In January 1761, trouble began for the newlywed couple, Christopher and Eliseba Beeler, when Eliseba encouraged her husband to draw up a will to avoid any future conflicts over his vast estate. After all, this was Christopher's third marriage, and he was a very wealthy man; there were quite a few people in his life who could make a claim for an inheritance. Beeler had fathered three children with his first wife; he also had three children from his second wife; there were also his stepchildren, fathered by Hans Michael Schüle; and, of course, there could be future children with his new wife, Eliseba. Drawing up a will was a prudent decision, especially given Beeler's unusual situation. This, however, drew the ire of a deceased wife. In spirit form, she began to haunt Eliseba.

A thirty-nine-page pamphlet published by the Ephrata Cloister in 1761, *An Exacted Relation on the Appearance of a Disembodied Spirit*, told Eliseba's story. The Pennsylvania Historical Society owns the only known surviving copy of the pamphlet. Klaus Wust translated the pamphlet and had it printed in the appendix of his 1977 book *The Saint-Adventures of the Virginia Frontier: Southern Outposts of Ephrata* under the title "The Ghosts of Longmarsh Run: The Three Wives of Christopher Beeler." The *Chronicon* has an abbreviated version of Eliseba's story; quoted below is part of the tale:

> *It happened in January 1761, that as this third wife of the man mentioned (his name was C.B.), was slumbering, an old woman appeared to her, who, according to the description given by her, must have been the above-mentioned widow. She took hold of the arm of said third wife, and placed her on a chair, and that part of the arm which she had taken hold of was blue for several days. Then she said to her: "Don't go away, but remain here with my husband, I am an old woman and do not mind it; I shall go away again; you are the third and legitimate wife. And because you are good to my children, I shall reveal everything to you, for you will not be here much longer. Go into the kitchen about the twelfth hour; there behind the tin closet you will find money." Afterwards she and her husband searched the kitchen and found there £3 hidden, in paper money. After this the spirit played a strange comedy with this person for four weeks, so that she thought it would cost her life, as she suddenly spit half a pint of blood. Every night the spirit revealed some of the money which the woman had during her lifetime purloined from her husband, and which was found in the places where she had hidden it. But it appears that the*

spirit must have been greatly under the influence of a fierce temper, for whenever it was not obeyed, it would tear the clothes from the body of the wife; and that was a common thing. If she rode behind her husband, her shoes and stockings were taken off her feet while sitting on the horse. Did she go to a neighbor, it always cost her part of her dress, which was torn; but if she remained at home, there was a continual racket all around the woman. Sometimes all the books were thrown down from the shelf, and hardly was this done when the tea-service followed and was broken to pieces. At length the report of these strange matters spread over the whole country, and a messenger, B. by name, was sent from Winchester to inform himself accurately about the thing. He spent the night there; but during the night the spirit rioted in throwing, knocking and pounding so that the afore-named B. commenced to curse on his couch, which so exasperated the spirit that it dragged the couch on which three persons were lying around the room, though B. resisted with much force. Then the spirit took hold of his arm and tried to twist it, whereupon he cried out in fear: "Lord Jesus, what is this?" Now the spirit fell down upon its knees before him, pushed him back with both its hands, and disappeared.

They several times heard the spirit utter the word Conestoga, at which place they had formerly lived; and because the wife was always seized by the arm by the spirit they interpreted it to be the spirit's meaning that they should go to Conestoga. In this they were not deceived, for as soon as they had resolved on this move two spirits appeared; the last stood behind the first and was quite tall and lean, which made them think it was C.B.'s first wife. Whenever the first said to his wife, "Come!" the second would stand behind and beckon with its hand that they should come and behaved very devoutly. After the wish of the spirit in regard to the journey was divined it plainly told them the whole affair, namely, that they were to go from Ephrata to Conestoga; about the twelfth hour of the night they should enter the great hall over the church, and to this place Conrad (this was the Superintendent whom the deceased during her lifetime had highly esteemed), Nagele, her husband, and a Sister who had long ago died (most likely Anna Eicher), should also come; it and Catharine (the first wife of said C.B.) would also appear, for they had died unreconciled with each other. Then the following two hymns were to be sung: "Oh God and Lord," and "Dearest Father, I Thy child." After this they should clasp each other's hands, but she should put her hand on them and say: "Christ is the reconciliation of us all; may he help you and forgive you your sins and wash you with his blood." On this journey to Ephrata it *was observed that as often as she tarried longer than necessary the spirit became uneasy and threw her shoes towards the door; and in Lancaster it also tore her clothes in sight of all the people in the tavern.*

When Eliseba, her stepson Joseph and Christopher Beeler arrived at the Ephrata Cloister, the superintendent, who was the cloister's founder, Johann Conrad Beissel, was away on business. Not wishing to meddle in such an odd affair, the Brothers at the cloister refused to get involved and instead sent for Beissel. Beissel refused to go at first but had a change of heart and returned to Ephrata. An attempt to reconcile the disembodied spirit with the living took place during a meeting on February 3. According to the *Chronicon*:

The meeting was held February 3rd; it began at the eleventh hour of the night and lasted two hours. Besides those three persons from Virginia, eighteen from Ephrata were present, and among them those whom the deceased had especially named; but the chief person with whom the spirit had had to do refused to be present until she was at last persuaded to it after much trouble. The meeting was commenced by reading the last chapter of James, and after the first hymn had been sung, all knelt down; but when the spirit was mentioned in the prayer, strange emotion took possession of her, and she was seized by great fear, so that her husband and step-son had to support her. It was noticed at the time that her neckerchief became sprinkled with blood while they were on their knees; there were thirty drops, but where the blood came from did not become evident. This was the only extraordinary circumstance that happened at this meeting, for the spirit did not appear according to promise.

In the pamphlet, Joseph Beeler, Eliseba's stepson, said of the blood on the neckerchief:

It was noticed at this moment that her neckerchief became suddenly stained with blood. There were thirty drops. Someone pointed the blood out to her as it was still fresh. Then she wiped off several drops. Despite all efforts nobody could discover where the blood had come from. My father opened the front of her shirt to see if it had come from within, but he could not perceive anything except a few drops that had penetrated to the undershirt. We are keeping the neckerchief, and each and every drop can be seen on it. Most amazing is the fact that the sprinkling blood had spared both apron and shirt. No person could have sprinkled it with such precision.

A poster produced by Katherine Milhous for the Work Projects Administration. *Public domain image. Wikimedia Commons.*

The spirit did not appear in the ceremony as predicted, and living stand-ins filled the void. From the pamphlet:

> *At last it was thought advisable that the two daughters, the one by the first wife, the other by the second wife, should perform the reconciliation instead of their mothers. They clasped their hands, and the said Eliseba Beeler, acting as priestess, spoke the words over them which the ghost had placed in her mouth. Thereupon all knelt down again, and after the prayer was said, the ghosts made off. Nobody had seen anything but we all heard how the window opened and closed again. My stepmother kept on looking to one side. She expressed surprise that we had not seen them as they had just flown away in the shape of two doves.*

The ritual must have met the approval of the disembodied spirit of Christopher Beeler's deceased wife; the written record shows that after the ceremony, the ghost did not appear to Eliseba again. Sometime afterward, Christopher Beeler moved to his property on New Creek, near present-day Keyser, West Virginia, and one of his sons took possession of the land along Long Marsh Run. Beeler supported his children and grandchildren in his last will, written in 1773. Money from the sale of Beeler's house in Alexandria went to the Sisters at the Ephrata Cloister when he died.

10
Other Strange Tales

All a skeptic is is someone who hasn't had an experience yet.
—*Jason Hawes*

At this point in the book, various hauntings from all over the county have been discussed at length. Actual eyewitnesses graciously provided many of the stories recounted in previous chapters. People with stories to tell were very forthcoming; in fact, too many were received to include them all in the book. A few favorites that did not fit neatly into the previous chapters have been saved for this final chapter, as well as a couple of stories obtained from other sources. Their place at the end of the book in no way diminishes their impact; many of the tales to follow are as chilling as anything presented thus far.

The Smoky Figure

Jewell Lilly moved to Clarke County in the late 1980s. After spending several years in an old farmhouse in Berryville—a house that had its share of unexplained activity—she moved into a home along Briggs Road. Immediately after moving in, strange things started happening. Loud knocking sounds emanated from the walls; doors would open and shut on their own; the lights would turn on and off; light bulbs were constantly blowing out. In fact, light bulbs were blowing out so frequently that it became quite expensive to keep enough on hand. This activity, as annoying and frightening as it was, would pale in comparison to the things she would soon encounter.

"I remember after moving in just sitting on the couch in the living room and getting this overwhelming feeling that something didn't want me there," Jewell recalled. "I felt like I needed to get up and leave. Of course, I didn't."

Shortly after having the overwhelming feeling of needing to leave, but deciding to stay put, the strange activity in the home took a nasty turn. Late one night, the sound of laughter next to her head woke Jewell from her slumber. "It was a man's voice," she said. "He seemed to be making fun of me."

By far, the scariest place in Jewell's home was the basement. Even her pets were afraid and refused to go down the steps. One evening, she and her son needed to retrieve something from the basement. As soon as they opened the door, the light turned on by itself. "I just shut the door and turned back around," she recalled. "There was no way we were going down there!"

Perhaps the most frightening incident in the home occurred when her son, between fifteen and sixteen years old at the time, was playing video games in the basement with his friends. Jewell prefaced this story by saying that none of the boys had been drinking and there was no history of drug use among any of them. Jewell was on the couch watching television when the boys came thundering up the steps in a panic. "Now keep in mind, these were big boys," she said, "football-playing boys, big linemen."

While the boys were in the basement, glowing red eyes appeared on the wall. The eyes, or whatever they were, flew off the walls straight at them, and they fled in terror.

Jewell's son had another harrowing encounter in the home, this time in his bedroom. He woke up one night to find a "smoky figure" standing at the foot of his bed. Terrified, and not knowing what to do, he pulled his covers over his head. When he lowered the covers and looked out again, the figure was gone.

Jewell's house was built in 1965. From talking with several neighbors, she learned that a former owner of the home held weekly poker games in the basement. During a game in the late 1970s or early 1980s, one of the participants died of a heart attack. Armed with this knowledge, she began addressing the entity in her home by name and asked him to stop blowing out the light bulbs.

Jewell began to get used to the ghostly activity in her home, but it was still a nuisance, and she did ask the spirit to leave. Finally, some years later, a friend of hers, whom she described as a "strong male presence," asked the entity to leave her home. This did the trick; there has been no strange activity in the home since.

THE GHOST LIKES YOUR BALLOON

Jennifer Crane Oliver used to live in a small house across from the railroad tracks in Boyce. Built in 1962, the home lies along Virginia Avenue. Virginia Avenue is Route 666, an irony that has not gone unnoticed to Jen when she recounts her experiences in the home.

Jen believes that the spirit of a little boy is present in her former home. This little boy had a way of picking on her youngest daughter—in much the same way that little boys who are living pick on young girls. She shared a story in which the ghostly boy stole her daughter's balloon.

"We had gotten back from Hibachi Grill in Winchester," recalled Jen. "They had given both the girls balloons."

A most unusual choice for a road number—666. *Courtesy of the author.*

After arriving at home, the girls took their balloons inside with them and began getting ready for bed. Both girls tied their balloons to their clothes and came downstairs to say goodnight to their parents.

While saying goodnight to the youngest girl, Jen noticed something strange: "When I went to kiss her goodnight, I felt a fan of air. It was like a literal wall of air had gotten in between us."

When the youngest kissed her father goodnight, she realized her balloon was missing. The family searched all over the house to find the missing balloon—the same search that countless parents have carried out when an upset child has lost something dear to them. Unfortunately, Jen and her family were unable to find the balloon, and the little girl went to bed crying.

The next morning, after Jen kissed her husband goodbye as he headed off to work, she turned around and saw the balloon in the middle of the living room. She told her daughter, "I guess the ghost must be done playing with your balloon."

"Is the ghost a girl or a boy?" the little girl asked.

The answer to this question was forthcoming.

Jen had long felt that a childlike spirit inhabited the home. She was often awakened to cries of "mom," but when she would check on her girls, they were always fast asleep. The "mom" cry even occurred on a night when her daughters were away for the weekend.

One day, Jen caught a glimpse of a little boy in her hallway. "He was wearing powder blue pajamas with fire trucks on them," she vividly recalled. "They don't make that style of pajamas anymore, it was something you'd see in the sixties or early seventies."

The boy walked into a room, and Jen followed him. When she entered the room, the mysterious boy had vanished.

"I never had any scary experiences in the house," she said. "I think he might have been attracted to me because I'm a mother."

"HE IS CALLING ME"

The mother of a boy who had a frightening experience years ago recounted a strange story. The event took place in 1992 in a patch of woods in Boyce where the Roseville Downs subdivision now sits. Her son and three other adolescent boys were in the woods, and they were playing with a crystal ball. Four boys in the woods with a crystal ball—what could possibly go wrong?

At some point, one of the boys fell down; more likely than not, he passed out. The other three boys tried hard to wake him, to no avail. They went as far as to stuff snow down his clothes in hopes that the cold would shock him into waking up. When the boy finally came to, something was wrong—very wrong. He was speaking in a guttural voice, growling like an animal. Worst of all, his eyes had turned red!

In his deranged state, the kid took off running through the woods. The other boys chased him down and subdued him, and he finally became himself again.

That night, one of the boys who lived on East Main Street, near the railroad tracks, had a sleepover at his house, and the three other boys stayed over. Sometime after eleven o'clock, three of the boys woke up and realized that their friend who had had the strange experience earlier in the day was sleepwalking down the street, headed toward the railroad tracks. The group managed to chase him down and wake him up. When they asked him what was going on, he said, "I had to go, he is calling me."

What happened in the woods that day? Did the boys unwittingly conjure something while they were playing with the crystal ball? Did something happen similar to the many tales of kids playing with Ouija boards who inadvertently unleash something terrible—something beyond our understanding?

Maybe there is a more natural explanation: Perhaps the boy suffered from a physical or even a mental condition. Something such as this could certain frighten a group of young boys and even make them believe something supernatural had taken place.

There is no way to know what happened all those years ago, but it is fair to wonder: If something from beyond our natural world was in the woods that day—and it tried reaching the boy later that night—could it still be on the loose today?

A Soldier at the Foot of the Steps

An anonymous woman from White Post tells the story of her husband, skeptical about the existence of ghosts, who had a change of heart after experiencing the paranormal firsthand. The couple rented a home for a year on Berrys Ferry Road. It was a very old house, which she believed was built in the late 1800s or early 1900s.

Many bizarre things happened while the couple lived in the home, most notably, the sound of phantom footsteps on the stairs. The footsteps eventually stopped, but only after the husband saw something strange. One morning, at the bottom of the stairs, stood a fully uniformed soldier, probably from the time of the Civil War. It seems the soldier did not want to frighten anyone; he simply waved to the husband and disappeared.

The anonymous storyteller claimed that things took a really strange turn as the family was moving out of the house. "When we were moving out it was much worse," she said. "Lights began to flicker, and things got weirder."

She recalled being surprised by a strange voice. "One evening my son and I were in the kitchen packing and someone, who sounded like a young girl, said 'hello' as clear as day."

When the moving truck was packed and ready to go, the woman and her son went to the new house while the husband stayed behind to take care of some last-minute details. Something happened during that time that shook him to the core. His wife recounted, "To this day he will not tell me details, but the look on his face that day said enough." He did tell her that the lights were flickering, and that he heard voices. He also refused to go back to the house even to drop off the keys.

One must wonder, what did the voices say that disturbed him to such a degree?

An Old-Timey Poltergeist?

Poltergeists—ghosts or supernatural entities capable of affecting the physical world by moving objects—were made famous by the 1982 classic horror film *Poltergeist*. But, did you know that long before Steven Spielberg conceived the idea for the film, poltergeists were busy throwing objects and making people uncomfortable in their own homes right in the heart of the Shenandoah Valley?

Residents near Old Chapel were on edge in 1895 when someone, or something, subjected the home of James Peyton to a bout of stone throwing. On August 13, 1895, the *Richmond Dispatch* reported:

Mysterious Flight of Stones

The people living in the neighborhood of the "Old Chapel" have been very much stirred up over the mysterious stoning of the house of James

Historic Old Chapel is the oldest Episcopal church in continuous use west of the Blue Ridge. The Burwell family cemetery is located on the grounds. *Courtesy of the author.*

> *Peyton for several days and nights. At first the stones were thrown at night, but recently in the broad daylight they have fallen upon the house, coming from nowhere, so far as can be seen. Besides thoroughly alarming the inmates, the missiles have broken nearly every pane of glass in the house. A day or two ago a large stone fell in the centre of the dinner-table while the family were at dinner. Mr. Peyton, who is a very respectable man, says he has not an enemy in the world, so far as he knows, and can assign no cause for this mysterious attack on his dwelling. A number of persons have watched the premises, hoping to catch someone throwing the stones, but have been unable to see no one, or to find the source of this strange attack.*

For weeks the rock attacks continued; evidence of a prankster could not be found, nor could any source for the flying stones be located. It was as if something, rather than someone, was behind the episodes of stone hurling. Things would only get worse and take an even sharper turn into the world of the strange. Five weeks after the aforementioned article ran, the *Shepherdstown Register* reported:

Haunted Clarke County, Virginia

A Much Haunted House

A Berryville dispatch to the Richmond Dispatch *of last week, says: The mystery as to the stoning of the residence of James Peyton, in Clarke County, remains still unsolved, and the missiles continue to pelt the dwelling, to the annoyance of the family and the wonder of the neighborhood. At first the matter was looked upon the community at large as hardly worthy of notice, but as time passes and the attacks continue and it seems impossible to arrive at a correct solution of the mystery the county is becoming and more excited over it, and groups of persons may be frequently discussing the matter and wondering at the probable cause of the disturbances. Lately the missiles have not been limited to stones, but tin cups, buckets, etc., have been thrown about the rooms, clothing and other articles have been unaccountably removed from one part of the house to the other, articles laid down for a moment have been spirited away, only to reappear as mysteriously, and other strange and unaccounted for circumstances keep the family in a constant state of uneasiness and alarm. The missiles thrown seem controlled by no law, but fall at the most unexpected moments, and from all directions. At one time it was thought that a cornfield, the only possible shelter nearby, concealed the attacking persons—if persons they are—who are responsible for the occurrences, and not some emissary from the spirit world unduly incensed against the persecuted family, but repeated examinations of the ground in the corn-field have failed to disclose any tracks or other evidences of the presence of human beings. Again, others were of the opinion that some member of the family, actuated either by a spirit of malice or the desire to create a sensation, was responsible for the trouble, but all efforts to detect such a one or to attribute the disturbances to human agency have so far been unsuccessful, and the mystery grows more perplexing and the alarm of those persons who are believers in the supernatural becomes greater as the days go by.*

Who, or what, was pelting the house with rocks? The easiest solution would be to write off the episode as the work of a prankster. But, with the objects moving within the home, and given the amount of paranormal activity that has been observed throughout Clarke County, would it be all that surprising for a rock-throwing phantom to be roaming the area?

AFTERWORD

As I passed a certain point on one of the isolated roads I was suddenly engulfed in fear. I stepped on the gas and after I went a few yards my fear vanished as quickly as it came. I continued to drive, eventually returning to the same spot. And again, a wave of unspeakable fear swept over me.
—*John Keel,* The Mothman Prophecies

One of the scariest things I remember happened when I was eighteen years old. I was alone, standing on the banks of the Potomac River, catfishing on a cold and starry autumn night. It was getting near 1:00 a.m. when I saw a gray streak, or flash, out of the corner of my eye. "Oh, s—," I muttered to myself.

My heart sank, and I began to take short, rapid breaths; I had trouble swallowing, and my skin turned cold and clammy; my stomach knotted up, and my heart beat so fast that I thought it might leap out of my chest. My legs started to quake—it felt like I was standing on rubber bands. In spite of myself and my panicked condition, I managed to reel in my lines. Scared out of my wits or not, being eighteen, living on my own and working for a seven-dollar-an-hour wage, I wasn't about to leave my prized fishing gear behind. Once my lines were in, I slung the chicken livers from the hooks, fixed the hooks into the eyelets on the poles, swiped my tackle box and made a beeline for my 1984 Mazda B2000 pickup.

You see, I was fishing along Balls Bluff Battlefield. This was back in the early 1990s, when you could park close to the river and walk down and fish

Afterword

at night without getting into trouble—long before runaway development swallowed up the Leesburg area and well before Balls Bluff became a popular destination for nature walks. At any rate, whatever I saw out of the corner of my eye (if I really even saw anything at all) was, in my estimation, a Confederate ghost. Ghost sightings are commonplace at the battlefield, where the Union suffered a decisive defeat, with many retreating soldiers drowning in the Potomac. So, having all of the ghost stories in mind that I had heard in my teenage years, I ran up the hill as fast as my legs would take me. I started my truck and threw it in reverse. I popped the clutch and stomped the gas, slinging mud and gravel as I fishtailed out of there. I could not have been happier when Route 15 came into view!

As scared as I was as an eighteen-year-old at Balls Bluff, it doesn't compare to a muggy summer night at Ebenezer Church well over twenty years later. This is saying a lot; I'm certainly no stranger to spooky places.

It did not phase me when my wife screamed and went running, dropping my new iPhone on the ground, as I posed for a picture in front of the White Oak Cemetery sign in Gatlinburg, Tennessee. On this bitter-cold, moonless December night, the apparition of a soldier appeared behind me as my wife was snapping the picture. I got a chuckle from the encounter, but honestly, I was a bit upset that we failed to capture an image of the ghostly photobomber. I've only been to Ebenezer Church a couple of times; I can tell you, though, not once did I laugh when I was there.

When I visited the Stanley Hotel in Estes Park, Colorado, I experienced something very strange during a ghost tour. The guide took our group into a room thought to harbor several spirits, some of which were children. Once we entered the room, we all sat down, and the guide instructed us to sit in complete silence. Then she turned off the lights. We sat in the heavy silence and pitch black for about ten minutes, during which time I observed a burst of purple-colored light followed by a bouncing sphere about the size of a softball, also purple in color. The purple sphere moved in a way that defied both physics and logic. Although the appearance of mystery lights and orbs were commonplace in that room, I explained away what I was seeing as my eyes playing tricks on me in the heavy, almost oppressive darkness. Then something happened that I could not dismiss so easily. I felt a sudden weight on my legs and pressure against my chest. I began to get hot, and the room suddenly felt stuffy. It felt as if a kid was sitting on my lap—a kid too big and too heavy to sit on an adult's lap. I also felt uncomfortable, like when a child sits on your lap and it is a little too hot and humid for the two of you to be comfortable—think of a midsummer baseball game. This feeling continued for what felt like a couple of minutes. When the weight finally came off of me, the stuffiness left, followed by a sharp blast of frigid air. Throughout all of this, I felt a bit uneasy, but I was never frightened.

I have been to more creepy places than I can even recall—most of these places *should* be much more frightening than Ebenezer Church. Thinking back to a visit to the Trans-Allegheny Lunatic Asylum in Weston, West Virginia, a wheelchair in the hallway turned itself completely around while I ducked into one of the rooms for a look. That was a bit unsettling. I've heard a lot of stories from there of an invisible force blamed for scratching and pushing people down during their visits. My wife even took a picture of a horrifying entity that must have been right beside me without my knowing. The asylum is definitely creepy; but all in all, it didn't scare me too bad.

I could keep going down a long list of well-known haunts that I have visited, but I believe I have made my point—I think Ebenezer Church is as creepy as anywhere. This also includes various cemeteries and Indian burial mounds I have visited in the dead of night; peering into dark caves looking for signs of mountain lions; trekking through shadowy, overgrown stretches of forest hoping to get a glimpse of the hide-and-seek champion, Bigfoot.

"So, what happened at Ebenezer Church?" you are probably wondering. The answer: nothing. Absolutely nothing. Not one thing. Aside from some heavy spikes on my EMF meter and just a bad feeling in general, nothing out of the ordinary occurred. I did not even capture any orbs in my pictures. I just got scared. That's it—scared. But not like normal. No, this was an irrational fear that suddenly swept over me. It is almost impossible to describe the feeling. I will say, though, that I forced myself to hold it together. I walked to my car calmly rather than running through the woods like a bat out of hell as a terrified eighteen-year-old at Balls Bluff.

The legendary paranormal author and investigator John Keel often wrote of this type of irrational fear overtaking a person during paranormal encounters. It even happened to him in the late 1960s in Point Pleasant, West Virginia, when he was investigating the infamous Mothman. Keel was a bit ahead of his time; he pointed to sound waves as a potential explanation for irrational fear. He penned the following in his 1975 book *The Eighth Tower*:

> *Sound waves produce a variety of interesting effects on biological organisms, some of them similar to the effects of radio waves. A sound wave at just the right pitch can fill you with absolute terror even though you can't hear*

it. Ghosts, hairy monsters, and UFOs can apparently be accompanied by this kind of sound, creating unreasonable fear in humans and even stronger reactions in animals that can hear sounds that are beyond the range of human hearing.

Rich Daniels, a researcher whose primary area of focus is the study of the traumatic effects that witnesses often suffer after an encounter with a cryptid, believes, as many do, that the most famous cryptid of all, Bigfoot, might be capable of using infrasound. This, he believes, can account for the inability of witnesses to think clearly during an encounter. It also can explain other adverse effects of cryptid sightings, such as disorientation, nausea, being frozen in place and becoming overwhelmed by a crippling feeling of terror.

Throughout the paranormal community, infrasound is known as the "fear frequency." Daniels describes it this way:

Infrasound is classified as low frequency sound in the range below 20 Hertz which is below human auditory capacity. This low frequency sound is of little consequence to humans until it reaches the 90–100 decibel range. If you think of sound as toothpaste in a tube, Hertz represents how thick the paste is and decibels represent how hard the tube is squeezed to create the pressure to force the paste out. Human auditory range is comfortable around 500 Hertz, so none of us have actually "heard" infrasound, but people certainly feel it.

I worked for the massive defense contractor Raytheon for many years. In the mid-2000s, the company was working on the development of nonlethal weapons, mostly for the military or law enforcement to use for crowd control. Nearly all of the proposed weapons involved the use of sound waves. Among the weapons were the following: sonic bullets, or high-powered blasts of sound produced by antenna dishes between three and six feet in diameter; acoustic infrasound capable of long-distance travel and able to pass through automobiles and buildings; an acoustic "squawk box" that can direct a concentrated sound beam through a crowd and target a specific individual; and acoustic teleshot, a sonic blast delivered by a twelve-gauge shotgun. In 2011, the company patented a riot shield that emits low-frequency waves. These are but a few examples.

This sound energy, in the form of low-frequency waves, some of which are able to penetrate buildings, can induce fear, disorientation, vomiting, fainting, extreme irritability and even organ damage.

Afterword

Neel V. Patel, writing for Inverse, a website that uses a rigorous scientific approach to analyze current trends and the culture at large, dipped his toe into the paranormal in an article titled, "Four Scientific Explanations for the 'Ghost' You Think You See." He began the piece by saying:

> *Let's pretend, for argument's sake, that ghosts are real. What, then, do you define as a ghost? If you believe paranormal activities can have a supernatural cause, then you're basically saying you believe in the world of spirits and demons and a universe that is not limited to the laws of physics.*
>
> *But let's be real here: Ghosts don't exist. These apparitions aren't manifestations of a spiritual world and can be explained by the natural laws that govern the universe.*

Patel went on to offer infrasound as one possible scientific explanation for the existence of ghosts. This is a far cry from the idea that infrasound can accompany ghosts and strange creatures, but it nevertheless helps explain the effects on witnesses who have an encounter. Says Patel:

> *There are some frequencies of noise humans can't actually hear, but that doesn't mean the effects go unnoticed. Infrasound refers to the sound emitted at ultra-low frequencies. Although infrasound cannot be heard, the vibrations they cause have tangible effects—wind turbines and traffic noises can create residual infrasound that can induce feelings of disorientation and aberrations in blood pressure and heart rate that are in line with what happens when one is stressed or panicked...or the same frightful effects one might expect when they chance upon a ghost.*
>
> *Quite a few papers have attempted to make the connection between infrasound and ghosts—and it seems clear thus far that low-frequency vibrations cause some kind of physical effects on the body.*

I do not agree with Patel's assertion that ghosts do not exist and that infrasound can explain them away. I do tend to believe, however, that infrasound occurs during some paranormal encounters. And this does have an adverse effect on the mind and body. How can this occur? The answer to that question is well above my paygrade. If I were to hazard a guess, I would say that ghosts are composed of some sort of energy; we know (or think we know) this energy is capable of moving objects, making audible sounds and presenting itself in the form of an apparition. With that in mind, is it too much to believe that this energy could also produce low-frequency sound waves? Maybe even as a side effect?

I like this idea, and it explains a lot. It can account for the sudden rush of fear I felt at Ebenezer Church. Heck, the more I think of it, it might even explain my misadventure at Balls Bluff in 1992. After all, there is no way a guy like me would ever scare himself silly with thoughts alone. Not a chance!

I am glad that pioneers of the paranormal have studied and written about the role that infrasound might play in certain situations. I'm also glad for another thing: if I want a paranormal experience, I don't have to go far. Sure, it might be sexier to explore a haunted penitentiary several hours away. Famous hotels across the country and haunted asylums also have their appeal. But who needs to spend the time or the money? There is more haunted history right here in the Shenandoah Valley than most places, and there are plenty of ghosts nearby. Haunted Clarke County is full of them.

SELECT BIBLIOGRAPHY

Books

Annual Report of the American Anti-Slavery Society. New York: American Anti-Slavery Society, 1861.
Bates, Samuel P. *History of Pennsylvania Volunteers, 1861–5, Vol. 2.* Harrisburg, PA: B. Singerly, State Printer, 1871.
Gold, Thomas Daniel. *History of Clarke County, Virginia and Its Connection with the War Between the States.* Berryville, VA: C.R. Hughes, 1914.
Hearn, Daniel Allen. *Legal Executions in Delaware, the District of Columbia, Maryland, Virginia, and West Virginia: A Comprehensive Registry, 1866–1962.* Jefferson, NC: McFarland & Company, 2015.
Hollis, Heidi. *The Hat Man: The True Story of Evil Encounters.* Milwaukee, WI: Level Head Publishing, 2014.
Keel, John A. *The Eighth Tower.* New York: Granada, 1975.
———. *The Mothman Prophecies.* New York: Tor, 1991.
Lamech and Agrippa. *Chronicon Ephratense a History of the Community of Seventh Day Baptists at Ephrata....* Translated by J. Max Hark, D.D. Lancaster, PA: S.H. Zahm, 1889.
Lancaster, Robert A., Jr. *Historic Virginia Homes and Churches.* Philadelphia: J.B. Lippincott Company, 1915.
Lee, Marguerite Du Pont. *Virginia Ghosts.* Berryville: Virginia Book Company, 1966.

Select Bibliography

Lepa, Jack H. *The Shenandoah Valley Campaign of 1864*. Jefferson, NC: McFarland & Company, 2003.

Mosby, John Singleton. *The Memoirs of Colonel John S. Mosby*. Edited by Charles Wells Russell. Boston: Little, Brown and Company, 1917.

Myers, Lorraine F., and Stuart E. Brown Jr. *The Annals of Clarke County, Virginia Volume IV*. Berryville: Virginia Book Company, 2002.

Ramage, James A. *Gray Ghost: The Life of Col. John Singleton Mosby*. Lexington: University Press of Kentucky, 2010.

Rothery, Agnes. *Houses Virginians Have Loved*. New York: Rinehart & Company, 1954.

Shaw, Adam. *Sound of Impact: The Legacy of TWA Flight 514*. New York: Viking Press, 1977.

Slave Narratives: A Folk History of Slavery in the United States from Interviews with Former Slaves. Washington, D.C.: Library of Congress, 1941.

Taylor, L.B. *The Big Book of Virginia Ghost Stories*. Mechanicsburg, PA: Stackpole Books, 2010.

———. *Haunted Virginia: Ghosts and Strange Phenomena of the Old Dominion*. Mechanicsburg, PA: Stackpole Books, 2009.

Willis, Carrie Hunter, and Etta Belle Walker. *Legends of the Skyline Drive and the Great Valley of Virginia*. Richmond, VA: Dietz Press, 1940.

Wust, Klaus G. *The Saint-Adventures of the Virginia Frontier: Southern Outposts of Ephrata*. Edinburg, VA: Shenandoah History, 1977.

Articles

Alexandria Gazette. "Hanged." January 27, 1905.

Baltimore Sun. "Another Insurrectionist Sentenced to Be Hung in Virginia." January 5, 1860.

Bee (Danville, VA). "92 Die in VA Crash." December 2, 1974.

Bradley, John. "Pushing William Penn's 'Holy Experiment' to Its Limits: Ephrata Cloister." *Pennsylvania Heritage Magazine* 22, no. 4 (Fall 1996): 14–23.

Clarke Courier (Berryville, VA). "Lippkin Resigned." January 18, 1905.

Eggert, Gerald G. "The Impact of the Fugitive Slave Law on Harrisburg: A Case Study." *Pennsylvania Magazine of History and Biography* 109, no. 4 (1985): 537–69.

El Paso Herald-Post. "Common Crash Factors Studied." December 3, 1974.

Gorn, Elliott J. "Black Spirits: The Ghostlore of Afro-American Slaves." *American Quarterly* 36, no. 4 (1984): 549–65.

Select Bibliography

Hamilton County Times (Noblesville, IN). "Hanging Was Like a Circus." February 2, 1905.

Levi, G. Kenneth. "Crow's Nest: New Use Saves Antebellum Beauty." *Clarke Courier* (Berryville, VA), April 26, 1990.

O'Connell, Doug. "They Still Come to See Where TWA 514 Crashed." *Progress-Index* (Petersburg, VA), December 1, 1975.

Playground Daily News (Fort Walton Beach, FL). "Crash Disrupts Classified Base." December 2, 1974.

Richmond Dispatch. "Mysterious Flight of Stones." August 13, 1895.

Rouse, Parke. "Wealthy Burwells Owned Chunk of Virginia." *Daily Press* (Newport News, VA), May 3, 1992.

Shepherdstown Register. "A Much Haunted House." September 19, 1895.

Sunday Star (Washington, D.C.). "One for One Hundred: Hitherto Unpublished Story of Thrilling Incident in Shenandoah Valley." July 22, 1922.

Times (Richmond, VA). "Mosby on Sheridan." January 27, 1895.

Underwood, J.C. "The Exile from Virginia." *New York Times,* July 10, 1856.

"The War Day by Day: Fifty Years Ago." *Boston Globe*, August 13, 1914.

Weekly Standard (Raleigh, NC). "Fugitive Slaves." September 4, 1850.

Wust, Klaus G. "German Mystics and Sabbatarians in Virginia, 1700–1764." *Virginia Magazine of History and Biography* 72, no. 3 (1964): 330–47.

Websites

Cahalan, Susannah. "This Is Where the Government Will Hide during a Nuclear War." *New York Post*, June 11, 2017. Accessed August 5, 2018. https://nypost.com.

Clarke Country Historical Association. Accessed July 18, 2018. http://www.clarkehistory.org.

Crocetti, Rachel. "When Your Dog Barks at Nothing, Are They Really Barking at Ghosts?" BarkPost. October 29, 2015. Accessed October 31, 2018. https://barkpost.com.

Daniels, Rich. "Infrasound: The Little We Really Know." National Cryptid Society. August 12, 2018. Accessed December 19, 2018. https://nationalcryptidsociety.org.

"Enclosure: William Taliaferro to Charles Lewis, 15 September 1757." Founders Online. Accessed July 22, 2018. https://founders.archives.gov.

French and Indian War Foundation. Accessed July 18, 2018. http://frenchandindianwarfoundation.org.

Select Bibliography

"Ghost Sightings." Ghosts of America. Accessed July 17, 2018. http://www.ghostsofamerica.com.

"Ghost Stories!" Houzz. Accessed August 7, 2018. https://forums.gardenweb.com.

"Ghost Stories from Virginia, United States: Page 1." Your Ghost Stories. Accessed August 7, 2018. http://www.yourghoststories.com.

Hebbard, Charles B., Mrs. "The Retreat." International Correspondence School/American School of Correspondence Archive. Accessed July 31, 2018. http://www.icsarchive.org.

"Historic Registers, Listings." Virginia Department of Historic Resources. Accessed September 7, 2018. https://www.dhr.virginia.gov.

MacFarlane, Scott. "Mt. Weather: Secret Govt. Facility Activated in April." NBC4 Washington, June 25, 2015. Accessed August 4, 2018. https://www.nbcwashington.com.

Marion, Casey. "Do You Believe in Ghosts?" Long Branch Historic House and Farm. Accessed March 3, 2019. https://www.visitlongbranch.org.

"National UFO Reporting Center Report Index by State/Province." National UFO Reporting Center. Accessed August 24, 2018. http://www.nuforc.org.

Patel, Neel V. "Chill Out, That's Probably Not a Ghost You See." Inverse. October 26, 2016. Accessed December 19, 2018. https://www.inverse.com.

Swain, Craig. "To the Sound of the Guns." To the Sound of the Guns. Accessed August 8, 2018. https://markerhunter.wordpress.com.

"Track UFOs." MUFON. Accessed August 24, 2018. https://www.mufon.com.

Pamphlets & Maps

Clarke County Government. *Clarke County, Virginia: Historic District Driving & Walking Tour Map.* Berryville, VA: Clarke County Historic Preservation Commission, 2014.

McCormick Civil War Institute. *Touring the Battle of Cool Spring.* Winchester, VA: Shenandoah University, 2018.

Shenandoah Valley Battlefields National Historic District. *Clarke County at War: Battlefield Driving Tour.* New Market, VA: Shenandoah Valley Battlefields Foundation, 2015.

Stanley, Steven. "Battle of Cool Spring, VA." Map. American Battlefield Trust. Accessed August 7, 2018. https://www.battlefields.org.

240th Anniversary Celebration. Berryville, VA: Berryville Baptist Church, 2012.

About the Author

Michael D. Hess was born in the southwestern Virginia town of Richlands in 1973. His family relocated to Loudoun County in the mid-1980s, and in 2006, he moved to Stephens City and married his wife, Stefanie, a Clarke County native. Hess works full time as an engineering technologist and is the self-published author of four paranormal and cryptozoology-themed books. Hess keeps busy hiking all over the Shenandoah Valley, traveling with his wife and adult children and researching unexplained phenomena.

Visit us at
www.historypress.com

www.ingramcontent.com/pod-product-compliance
Lightning Source LLC
Chambersburg PA
CBHW042143160426
43201CB00022B/2396